D1745624

FACING
THE MUSIC

ACC. No: 05264947

FACING
THE MUSIC

HANNAH
SPEARRITT

ЯENE
GADE

RENEGADE BOOKS

First published in Great Britain in 2023 by Renegade Books
This paperback edition published in 2024 by Renegade Books

1 3 5 7 9 10 8 6 4 2

Copyright © 2023 by Hannah Spearritt

The moral right of the author has been asserted.

Unless otherwise noted, all photographs courtesy of the author

Lyric on page 230 from 'S Club Party' by Hugh Atkins,
Mikkel Eriksen, Tor Erik Hermansen and Hallgeir Rustan.
Copyright © Polydor/19 Recordings Inc.

'S Club' is a registered trademark of XIX Entertainment

All rights reserved.
No part of this publication may be reproduced, stored in a
retrieval system, or transmitted, in any form or by any means, without
the prior permission in writing of the publisher, nor be otherwise circulated
in any form of binding or cover other than that in which it is published
and without a similar condition including this condition being
imposed on the subsequent purchaser.

A CIP catalogue record for this book
is available from the British Library.

Paperback ISBN 978-0-349-13103-0

Typeset in Berling by M Rules
Printed and bound in Great Britain by
Clays Ltd, Elcograf S.p.A

Papers used by Renegade Books are from well-managed forests
and other responsible sources.

Renegade Books
An imprint of Dialogue
Carmelite House
50 Victoria Embankment
London EC4Y 0DZ

www.dialoguebooks.co.uk

Dialogue, part of Little, Brown Book Group Limited,
an Hachette UK company.

To my partner, Adam. Up, down, sideways, diagonal,
back to front, inside out, all over the place . . .
But we're still here!

Contents

A Note from the Author   1

1. Read All About It   7
2. Going Back in Time   15
3. In the Spotlight   41
4. 'Do You Know the Way to San Jose?'   47
5. Reach for the Stars   59
6. Full Disclosure   77
7. Welcome to Miami!   87
8. Goodbye, Paul x   107
9. Breaking Up Is Hard to Do   129
10. Connor and Abby   137
11. Storm in a B Cup   155
12. Fake News   191
13. Family Ties   199
14. Crossroads   211

Afterword   225
Acknowledgements   229
Resources   235
About the Author   239

A Note from the Author

When I was presented with the opportunity to write my life story, I wouldn't call it imposter syndrome per se, but the first thing that sprang to mind was, *Will anyone really be that interested in what I've got to say?* That being said, I do read autobiographies which, by and large, are great reads and full of surprises – and the trials and tribulations that people have often gone through in silence. So after some deliberation, and knowing that the comfort zone is a place to avoid like the plague, here we are.

Some people will read this and think, *The silly entitled cow, she got lucky and won the lottery, with a great career from a young age.* Some, I hope, might sympathise a little! What I have come to realise is that everything is relative, and just because you might have had good fortune – or what looks like a rosy existence on the face of it – doesn't mean you don't suffer at times just like everyone else does.

This is a snapshot of the more relevant events in my life; the story of Hannah Spearritt, or 'Hannah from S Club' ... The title I've come to accept that I'll probably never shake! Both are me, of course, but different versions of me that have existed across my four-and-a-bit decades on this planet, and both stories deserve to be told.

When I think about what has happened to me, to my partner, Adam, and to my family over the last few years, it's probably the perfect tonic to sit down, pick up a pen, talk to an editor and get my experiences down on paper. It was, and is still, quite surreal because I never saw myself writing a book – in fact, I had been against it in the past.

When people say that writing is a kind of therapy, I interpreted that as it simply being a cathartic process – but wow, it has been so much harder than just recounting my story. Laughter one minute, tears the next. As I was writing, I was starting to think that it was helping me come to terms with, and hopefully overcome, the long list of calamities and crises which have been my life for the past six or seven years. But then another tragedy hit us all.

Shortly into the process, we lost Paul. It was an unforeseen and devastating tragedy that broke all our hearts. The untimely, cruel loss of someone who I shared so much with – who was still so young, our long-time bandmate and a son and brother – has caused unbelievable anguish. Knowing that Paul is gone forever made writing this book a painful process, opening old wounds and revisiting memories that had been locked away for years.

As part of S Club, I was heavily in the spotlight. When the band started to experience success, that brought immense scrutiny to every aspect of my life. I want to explain why I walked away from that, and to clear up some falsehoods and rumours – all the conjecture said and written about me over the years.

This book is my thank you to my supportive family, and to my loving and understanding partner, Adam. It's also an acknowledgement of thanks to all those who continue to play a part in shaping my life or have done so, for however brief or long.

There has been a lot of fun and adventure in my time here so far, and there are also things from my past that I've needed to deal with. And so it's now time to play the record of my life and face the music. This is my story, my truth, with no holds barred – and a new approach of me telling people how it is, even if that makes me feel uncomfortable.

Thank you for picking up this book, and a huge thank you to all the fans who've stood by me over the years. I hope you like the book, and should you have been affected by any of the things I've been through, don't hesitate to message me on Instagram.

Enjoy!

Chapter One

Read All About It

Hello and welcome to my little journey I'm about to share with you.

This felt like the final piece of the puzzle in order to fully recover from the last decade – physically and emotionally, because both those aspects of your health go hand in hand. I'm going to be as open as possible about everything in this book and share my honest views on some of the major events of my life. I want to be as respectful as possible when discussing these events but, as the age-old saying goes, 'there are three sides to every story'. I also hope that my story is still interesting enough to keep you reading without the need for any tabloid-style sensationalism! I'll let you be the judge of that . . .

I'm going to start here by discussing the illness I have battled with on and off since 2013. Usually I prefer to only focus on the positive aspects of life, in part to make up for the time I lost to illness, I'm sure. But that does not change what happened, what I went through, or my responsibility to highlight the often-unknown potential risks that silicone breast implants carry.

A large part of what's gone on in my life has been dictated

by the experience of being ill, and it has been unspeakably challenging at times, which is why I haven't discussed it too much previously. I don't want to start or end this book on a negative but I also don't want this message to get lost in the middle. Hard times have taught me to tackle the toughest obstacles first, so I'll say my piece and then we can move on to brighter things!

Part of me hopes that explaining how hard it was will give me closure on the topic, and in turn lighten my load, so to speak. Perhaps if I talk you through what my reality was, and highlight the extent of just how bad things got for me, I can also do justice to explaining just how bad breast implant illness can be – and why it drove me right to the edge.

Although I've spoken before on the subject, in all the work that I have done on breast implant illness, there has unfortunately been a lot of content removed or not spoken about, and I feel it's my duty to shed some light on just how sick I was. A later chapter talks about the different aspects of the ordeal, but it doesn't focus on just how sick I felt. I've listed some of the symptoms of my experience, and I haven't delved too deep into the level of suffering – but make no mistake, my reality felt worse than a death sentence at times because I didn't know if it would ever end. And all the symptoms I've touched upon, I had pretty much the entire time.

There were times when I thought about ending it all. Lying awake with insomnia all night, not able to get up the next day and forced to lie in bed, exhausted and isolated, in unbearable pain and discomfort, is not something to look forward to, near on every day for four years. Never being able to plan anything, always letting people down, not being believed and looking like absolute shit the entire time. The only positive thing I can say about that period is thank God I didn't have the kids then – it would've all been too much.

No matter how small the risks – and they're not *that* small anyway – women should know *all* those risks before they get the surgery. I've been met with all kinds of statements in response to the topic of breast implant illness, and *all* implants leak eventually, so saying 'it won't happen to you' or 'my surgeon was just no good' is textbook denial. Even the surgeons themselves tell you to replace them after ten years anyway. The decision to opt for surgery carries a lot more potential consequences than the general consensus alludes to, that's for sure. If I had known the risks, I would never have even met a surgeon to discuss the procedure in the first place. To anyone reading this, I strongly recommend that you do your homework and consider if – like me – you might be one of the unlucky people whose body cannot tolerate silicone.

Whilst we're on the subject of difficult topics to talk about, I know that the question that's been on everyone's mind is what happened with the band. So, I didn't exactly just quit the tour – it's more complex than that, and involves many different layers.

As you will read in this book, and as I've just touched upon, the recent years have been hard for me – probably like they have been hard for so many other people – with Covid, illness, having two babies, not working, and the rest . . . When the chance of the tour came up, I was cautiously excited. But there were some issues surrounding it which concerned me. One being that Paul and I hadn't spoken in roughly eight years; the other being his mental wellbeing. On top of that, my daughter was recovering from a serious injury so I couldn't give the tour that much thought initially, and my health was suffering. I was exhausted all the time which was taking the fun out of everything.

When Paul passed away suddenly, it was a huge shock. He was someone that I had a close relationship with; a relationship that was very emotional and ended badly. At the start of the tour, we were being professional about it and wiping the slate clean, you could say. As touring often put the seven of us in the same room, that could have created some awkward circumstances – so we had to be able to be civil for the good of the band. I'm glad to say that it was turning out to be an overall positive process, and we'd seemingly put the past behind us . . . Then I got the shocking news of Paul's passing.

I'd not had a great start to the year and my health took a rapid downward turn. The combination of everything that had happened over the previous six months was overwhelming. Adam and the girls were suffering because of it, and I had to do a lot of soul searching. In fact, I heard one of the girls asking Adam in the next room, 'Is Mummy staying in bed today?', and I burst into tears. No matter how hard it was, I had to do something – anything – that might help.

My fans have always meant a lot to me, and I didn't want to let them down – especially as I suspected it might be the last time – but I had to take time out because I was really struggling. I had also signed a book deal earlier in the year, before committing to the tour, and that had now become a very different prospect. I didn't feel like I had a clear path ahead of me anymore.

So there were many different reasons for me not doing the

tour. Some personal, some business, but it ended up just not being possible. And for that I am truly sorry to the fans who were so disappointed. Was it because of Paul's death? No. Tragic as it was, his family openly supported the tour going ahead, and he wouldn't have wanted to stand in the way.

S Club was a huge part of my life and always will be. But I'm a very different person now to who I was when we first formed. Life is always a work in progress and I've worked extremely hard over the last few years – and have been extremely hard on myself, I hasten to add. Personal circumstances that may not have got in the way of me as a young happy-go-lucky girl, or may not have been a priority previously, are now more important to me. Finally, it's time for me to navigate my life in a way that feels true to myself.

Chapter Two

Going Back in Time

'm not entirely sure where my desire and love of performing came from.

My mum reckons it is in my genes. She said from the moment I arrived I was full of natural confidence and had no fear.

Her great-grandmother performed on the stage in the old music halls of the day. And my nanny – my mum's mother – didn't have any money, what with it being wartime and everything, but she taught herself to play the piano and tap dance.

Apparently when practising her tap dancing she'd roll the carpet up because she could actually get a good sound from the floorboards, so maybe Mum's right and there is something in the old genes after all.

My dad can also hold a tune and I love hearing him sing.

But my parents were about as far from pushy stage parents as you could get.

They've given me endless support, guidance, praise and encouragement, but they wisely let me choose my own path.

Looking back at the pictures of my childhood, I definitely wasn't a shy, retiring three-year-old.

I was always adventurous and I had my own mind, especially when there was something I wanted.

Interestingly, I see those elements and other similar traits of mine in both my daughters.

My youngest, Tora, who is two, reminds me of myself so much, both facially and in her character.

I grew up in a detached house near the seaside in a village called Gorleston, near Great Yarmouth, with my mum, Jennifer, a retired hospital phlebotomist, and dad, Michael, an offshore navigation engineer.

Many years earlier, at a disco dance, my parents met and fell in love.

No one wants to know about their parents getting it on, but my young dad must have impressed my mum with his two-step disco shuffle on the dance floor and, well, the rest is history.

They married in their early twenties. I love my parents' wedding photo.

My mum's hair is parted straight down the middle – she looked beautiful – and it epitomises my favourite fashion era – the 70s. Three children followed with plenty of space in between to enjoy each child. I arrived last, on 1 April 1981.

Mum said I was a well-behaved, happy baby who rarely cried.

Our home was a normal-sized house in an ordinary street: the same you'd find in any other English seaside town, I suppose.

But it did have something special, and that was its garden; I loved it, and it was my dad's pride and joy.

It was quite deep and split in two with a hedge. You could

exit the conservatory out into the part of the garden that took you right to the back, where there was an orchard full of apple trees.

It was heaven to a kid. I'd run around and shake them to make the fruit fall to the ground.

Dad grew blackberries and had a vegetable patch where he'd grow lots of yummy things like garden peas.

They were my favourite thing to eat, fresh from the pod, and his new potatoes were amazing too.

Even to this day, having had good fortune to eat in restaurants all over the world, I have never tasted any potatoes as good as the ones my dad grew.

It was a fruitful garden. Things would be growing there all the time, apart from in the winter, but in the spring and summer there were delicious fruits to snack on like strawberries, and we'd be outside every chance we got.

I have so many happy memories of playing with my friends there at weekends.

During warm summer days, we'd get out the blue plastic floor slide.

We'd take turns squeezing on loads of shampoo, hose it down with water to make it slippery, then go whooshing and skidding along as fast as we could in the bubbles.

My first best friend was a little girl from school called Madeleine Ball. I would wear a bright pink pom-pom skirt, Madeleine wore a bright blue one and for several years we were quite inseparable: racing around the school playground, climbing trees and probably getting into mischief.

My early years, which set the tone for the rest of my life, were pretty much about having a good time.

Maybe that's why the first memory I have was such an intense one as it involved being at a party and developing my first crush on a boy.

His name was Neil White.

It was my brother Stuart's eighth birthday party. I remember the table being laid out and all his friends gathered around the table to sing 'Happy Birthday'.

I don't remember what I said exactly, but I was insistent that my chair was directly next to Neil and I wanted to be close to him.

Why him? I genuinely have no idea. It's obviously not possible for a three-year-old child to actually fancy somebody, but that day I had been drawn to him.

I wouldn't have a clue what he looks like these days. I don't even think Stuart has heard from him since leaving school, but I have had a conversation with my brother about it because I find it bizarre that that memory in particular made such an intense impression that it remains stuck in my head decades later.

When we were kids, our mum spent time working at the telephone exchange, and it cracks me up even now when I hear her posh phone voice from all that time ago.

When you ring the landline at home, she still answers the telephone with a clipped style of speaking, going 'Hello, 3, 3, 9, 8, 2, 3, Jenny speaking.'

She seems to morph into a character from *Downton Abbey* when she's on the phone and we love to tease her about it.

Another favourite childhood memory was helping Dad as he worked in the garden. Just the smell of freshly cut grass instantly transports me back to that rosy garden and idyllic time.

There was a little patio when you went outside of the conservatory, and I remember a picture of me standing there helping my dad out: he is pottering about as usual, and I'm handing him some water in a little bucket.

Growing up, I was an absolute daddy's girl. I always wanted to be by his side when he was fixing stuff around the house and working in the garden.

He is retired these days, but until I was about eleven, Dad would often be working away from home, sometimes for up to four months at a time.

Now as an adult four months seem to go by in the equivalent of a week, but back then, pre internet and all the distractions we have today in our busy lives, four months could feel like forty years.

Throughout his thirties, Dad worked around the world in exotic places such as Bahrain, Kuwait, India and China as an offshore worker on the barges.

It was very well paid, but it was tough work, laying pipes on the ocean floor for the likes of Shell and other big oil and gas companies. In those days they didn't have GPS and relied upon shore stations relaying information to the ships.

He and Mum got through those long, lonely nights by writing romantic love letters to each other to keep the flames alive.

I also missed him like mad and got very upset when he was away, so when he was home I wanted to spend as much time as possible with him and relished the little chats we had.

Being around him I felt safe and secure, and he gave such good advice.

He is a very warm and nurturing man, and it is lovely to

see that continuing with his grandchildren when I take them home to visit.

When he stepped away from offshore contracting to spend time at home with us, he set up his own recruitment company and his weekends off were devoted to Mum and the family, or driving me to various classes and auditions, so I will always be grateful to him.

I think my sister Tanya caught the travelling bug from dad as she has been based out in the Far East for a number of years running a Pilates teaching business.

Another great aspect of that house was the fact I could jump the fence to school; I'd regularly risk tearing my uniform climbing over it into the playing field of the secondary modern that I attended – Lynn Grove Academy. Handy in the mornings when you fancied an extra five minutes' snooze, especially in winter when you didn't want to be walking further than you had to in the cold.

I don't remember the house as much as the garden, but there was a piano we all had lessons on. We had a snooker table in the games room off the lounge, and my bedroom was quite small and normal.

Mum wasn't one for letting us cover our walls with posters, so I remember my bed the most. Until I was about ten I collected teddy bears and had them lined up in descending-size order on the bed.

In the evenings, sometimes Stuart and I would chat to each other from our bedrooms by shining torches across the landing. We had codes for words using a number of flashes – our own special version of Morse code – and would signal to each other until whoever fell asleep first. It was great fun for us, but annoying for our sister Tanya, I expect, when she was trying to sleep.

I never spent that much time inside Tanya's room because she had a doll that I was really scared of – probably deliberately to deter me from borrowing her clothes!

I never really liked dolls. Even before Tanya's sinister-looking one came onto the scene, I had no interest in them.

My mum got me a doll once and I had an allergic reaction to it: so much so that I just stuffed it under my bed. I was really annoyed by it, and I still don't quite know why.

Nor did my poor mum. However, she got the message loud and clear that I was not going to be one of those little girls that sat quietly dressing up dolls to look pretty, and she never bought me another.

My daughter Tora is quite the opposite – she has a little Barbie that she adores, constantly chatting to her and making sure she's sat next to her wherever she goes.

This Barbie even comes to school in the car with us. It's very sweet really, the way she takes care of her.

Instead, as a kid, I preferred Stuart's toys – Action Man and Lego – all that fun stuff that boys get to play with.

But when I could brave the sight of the doll, I'd go into my sister's room to hang out, and as she was eight years older than me, she would use me as a guinea pig to practise hairstyles.

I'd have to sit still as she'd comb and brush my locks into the look of the day, and in the late 80s and early 90s people liked to experiment. I suppose it got me used to having my hair frequently changed for shoots and videos later in life when I joined the band.

Understandably, given our big age gap, I wasn't really into the same things as my sister.

By the time I was hitting my teens, she was twenty-one. So, I guess age sort of got in the way of us being super close growing up.

However, we are very close now as a family, and I partly have Tanya to thank for igniting my passion for performing.

She was into dancing, and she was a good choreographer. Mum and I think she should have set up her own dancing school because she had such a natural flair. But she didn't take that path.

She would choreograph a lot of the dance routines that we would learn at dance school and was a great support when I was preparing for shows.

She even took me along to an audition in London for a show called *Mini Pops* when I was about ten, and she got me ready for that audition by going over the dance routine with me so I would be perfect in my rendition of Madonna's 'La Isla Bonita'.

On our summer holidays abroad to Spain, Tanya often used to take a bunch of costumes with her and organise a little show for holidaymakers starring me and some of the other children staying at the resorts we were visiting.

I absolutely loved showing off in those dances, and it was all good experience for what was to come later – so thanks, Tanya.

Mum was the one who started me off with dance lessons when I was three. I think at first she saw it as a way for me to make friends, and something to help burn off my excess energy levels, as I was always on the go.

I asked her for her thoughts before writing this book, as I wanted to know if I wanted to dance of my own accord or if was I copying my big sister.

She thinks Tanya getting into things first helped me, but she says she knew there was always something there, like with my nanny and great-great-grandmother.

And when my parents bought their first video camera, I was a proper little show off, always urging them to 'film me!'

I'd have ballet and modern dance and tap lessons three to four times a week, and never missed a class at the June Glennie School of Dance.

June was quite an imposing presence in those days to a young child, and something of a taskmaster.

I still remember the first time I visited the school. It was tucked away behind a shop in one of these little lanes off the main town centre.

The enticing sound of tinkling music was echoing out from the top of the stairs, calling me up.

Holding tightly onto my mum's hand in trepidation, I shyly clambered up the stairs to the first floor, where I was introduced to June herself, and a roomful of little girls all in their frilly pink ballet clothes.

June had short grey hair, wore a very feminine long dress, and sounded extremely posh.

I was immediately fascinated.

We were shown to the changing rooms and Mum helped me into my new pink tutu and ballet slippers.

Despite not being a girly girl, I liked that tutu and seemed to pick up the positions quite quickly.

According to Mum, June told her that I was 'a natural'.

But I disagree; I wouldn't say I loved ballet to start with. I think falling in love with it came later, when I was performing in shows.

The aspect of the art form I was captivated by was the costumes and make-up when getting ready for a show.

The drill side of ballet was tough, but looking back I've always been grateful to have that in my locker, because I think the discipline I gained from hours and hours of repeating the same movements has stood me in good stead throughout my life.

Being born before the war, June was old school, shall we say, in her teaching methods. Her daughter Beth sometimes taught ballet, and she was soft and kind. But it was her other daughter whose lessons stood out, steely-eyed Sharon.

She was far stricter than her mother ever was when she stepped in to teach modern dance, and on those Fridays racing up the stairs to class, I'd think, *Please don't let it be Sharon teaching today.*

She had short dark hair, was sharp tongued, and everyone – and I mean everyone – was absolutely terrified of her.

She carried a stick in class that she would brandish with glee during floor work.

Oh my God, I dreaded it. She would poke you sharply with the bloody thing if she spotted even the slightest glimpse of a back arch.

I'd be pressing my back as flat as I could to the floor in fear of the injury she could inflict on me with that horrid stick.

Her catchphrase when she did it was, 'I could get a double-decker bus under that,' as she poked her stick.

I never wanted to do anything wrong in Sharon's classes, so

maybe there is something to be said for her archaic teaching methods.

Even now I squirm at the memory though, and I can still hear her telling me to tuck my pelvis in. But I also have her to thank for my good posture all these years later!

Weirdly, during dance lessons there I began to morph into a shy, retiring little girl who hung back, but on stage I'd transform into a completely different person and just shine in whatever role I was playing.

My hidden extrovert side seemed to come to life under the stage lights; in class I guess I was self-conscious.

Unfortunately, this behaviour caused resentment with the other pupils, who felt they were working harder in classes than me but not getting solo parts. Some of them complained to June, Sharon and Beth.

One day after class, June called my mother in for a chat and explained to her she would no longer be picking me for the next show due to me hanging back in lessons.

Mum pleaded my case to June, who knew that I would perform perfectly on the night, insisting 'you know Hannah can do it'. And I always did.

June passed away last year, aged ninety. I lost touch with the school years ago, but I'll never forget my time there.

It's difficult to pinpoint the lightbulb moment when I knew that I was going to have a career in the performing arts.

When you start learning to dance, you never know where it is going to take you.

But all these years later, Mum loves to tell the story of the time she took me to see the musical *Cats* by Lord Andrew Lloyd Webber and Sir Tim Rice, when I was just seven.

Unbeknown to my poor mother, before leaving the house I'd sneakily slipped on my leotard underneath my clothes.

During the show I pulled off my top to show her and the rest of the amused theatre aisle the special costume I was wearing in preparation to dance, 'just in case one of the cast is sick and I need to go on there and perform!'

So maybe the path for me to work in the entertainment industry was set in motion during that matinee.

However, it nearly didn't happen. When I was ten I announced to my parents one day that I was retiring from dancing.

Over breakfast, I turned to them and solemnly declared, 'I'm done. I don't want to do it anymore.'

They both looked at each other and back at me in shock and said, 'Done with what?'

'Dancing.'

I'd concealed from them that I had been gradually losing interest in dancing and was growing bored of having to take part in festivals, finding them time-consuming when I wanted to see my friends and do normal young-girl things on a weekend.

As I had just been getting on with it and going through the motions, naturally they didn't believe me at first when I told them I wanted to throw the towel in on dancing.

To begin with, Mum wouldn't hear of it, saying, 'You've been dancing since you've been three. You don't just pack up straight away.'

She wisely (mothers know best, right?) gave me an ultimatum: 'This might just be a whim. We'll give it six months. And if you still feel the same in six months, then yes, you can give it up.'

I insisted again: 'I want to play tennis, I love tennis. I have lost interest in dancing – I am absolutely done with it.'

And I *was* absolutely done with it.

I loved maths and music lessons at school – drama came later – but at that point PE was my favourite subject.

I guess I must have been pretty coordinated, and I'd always been sporty, winning sports player of the year at school, having been long-distance running, swimming and, of course, dancing from an early age.

So, it made sense to my parents for me to become involved with athletics and playing tennis and they thought, oh well, let her go for it.

However, there may have been another reason – one I didn't give them – for my passion for sports, and that may have been something to do with a certain hot, hot, young teacher called Mr Purnell, who arrived at our school to teach PE.

Newly qualified and oh so enthusiastic, I still remember the first time I laid eyes on him.

Dark hair, olive skin, real strong bone structure and build with a dazzling smile.

The image of him standing there in just his PE kit of white short shorts and a T-shirt in the sunshine is burned into my memory for ever.

I'd never seen anybody so good looking before, or so physical. Not even any of the pop singers at the time or actors in *Neighbours* or *Home and Away*, which other young girls were fans of.

And Mr Purnell has still got it now.

I bumped into him not that long ago and oh my God, he literally looks the same.

I think quite a few of us fancied him. We'd try to jazz up our plain uniforms of white shirt and navy skirt to look cooler. I'd roll my skirt up to be a bit shorter and tie my shirt up in a bid to look more womanly and grown up. Think Britney in '. . . Baby One More Time'.

During one of our netball matches, which he was refereeing, a blonde girl called Kelly and I both went for the ball at the same time in a bid to impress him.

But girls being typical girls when a guy is involved, we ended up scrapping – much to my shame today.

Having got each other's hair, we pulled at each other for absolutely ages, swinging ourselves around in circles and yanking handfuls of blonde strands from one another's scalps.

Neither would let go and back down, so we ended up rolling around on the ground until Mr Purnell could prise us apart.

I don't know how we weren't both bald by the end of it!

I don't think there were winners, just losers showing off for his attention; thankfully we made up later.

I continued to pursue PE, and when it came to playing tennis I became so proficient at the game – unintentionally – that by the following year I was selected to attend a two-week tennis camp in Sarasota, Florida, run by a top coach at the time. It was the sort of place where kids are hot-housed in the hope of making them future tennis champions.

To be honest, what I wanted was to go to Disney World, and this was the perfect way to do it. My parents kindly agreed and accompanied me over to the US to make a holiday of it.

They dropped me off at my duplex and when they came

back two weeks later to pick me up, I was speaking like a little American and whacking balls over the net like a young Steffi Graf – OK, slight exaggeration.

It was a lot of fun and Dad reckoned I was quite a good player, but I didn't have the burning desire to push myself at the game the way that you need to if you want to be a real success.

However, all of the sports I played and all the competitions I entered in tennis, athletics, dancing and netball gave me something I still draw on all these years later as an adult, and that is resilience.

When I am struggling with something, I look back on those times and know how to dig deep in the moment to gain the strength to keep going. It's always helped me, and I can't stress enough the importance of exercise and sport to a child's wellbeing.

When the weather was colder, we naturally spent more time inside the school on lunch breaks, and this is when all things drama and music crept into my life.

Hanging out in the music rooms was fun, and at breaktimes we used to just piss about in there and play on all the musical instruments available. My little group of friends and I would make up songs that must have sounded just awful.

But the best place in the whole school to be was the 'Drama Cupboard'.

Even though it was called a cupboard, it was actually like something from *The Lion, the Witch and the Wardrobe*, where you'd be transported into what felt like a totally magical world.

You'd push the door open and wade through all these

packed costumes to emerge into a hidden space where you could play dress up to your heart's content, hidden away from the rest of the world.

The soundproof room was behind the school stage and the ideal spot to hide away from our teachers, who couldn't see past all the clothes in it when they came searching for us.

To a kid it was pure heaven, and just the best place to hang out – especially when skiving off assembly.

I'd be in stitches with my friends, while the oblivious teachers and all the other poor sods at school were forced to sit through another of our headteacher Mr Bateman's tedious lectures and sing dull hymns.

We relished that sense of naughty playfulness we got from getting away with having fun during school assembly time.

And this may sound a bit weird, but the musty smell of old stage costumes is intoxicating to me.

There's nothing like it, because it takes me back to a very happy time with my friends, dressing up and pretending to be characters in little sketches we'd make up.

Acting for me is pure escapism, and all the time I spent hiding in that cupboard dressing up as other people and living in imaginary worlds was a way to forget about and heal from any troubles I had.

Mr Bateman's reputation was very strict. If you got in trouble you'd get called to his room, where you would receive a slap on the bum.

Thankfully I got away with my naughty behaviour and was spared this indignity, as my mother would have heard about it and I did not want to disappoint her.

Mum, maybe all of five feet and half an inch in her

slippered feet (don't forget the half inch, she says), was definitely the disciplinarian out of my parents. We weren't allowed to swear and I'd get told off at the dinner table for slouching or bad table manners. Sunday lunches were the worst, as I wasn't allowed to leave the table until I had eaten all my sprouts. I hated the horrible things, so our lunches would be very long, drawn-out affairs, as Mum insisted on piling them on my plate.

The general consensus seems to be that the youngest child has an easier time, but in my case that did not hold true. In my eyes, Tanya got away with a lot more stuff than me. I think my parents were stricter with me because maybe they thought as I was the youngest, I was more innocent, and they wanted to protect me for as long as they could.

Until she went back to working full time, Mum would always have dinner on the table at 5 p.m. sharp. I loved her cooking – especially after awful school dinners.

Mum and Dad – when he joined in cooking – had their staple meals, such as a fruity and fragrant chicken curry that I loved. Mum would put sultanas in it, and it was delicious.

She'd make batches of it, and growing up in the 80s and 90s, Tupperware ruled the kitchen.

Back then it was all the rage among the young mums to hold Tupperware parties – so our fridge and cupboards were filled with Mum's Tupperware boxes hiding all sorts of culinary surprises.

We were a musical house. Every morning when we woke up there was music playing, which I always loved. Dad would play a lot of Cat Stevens and Fleetwood Mac, which definitely impacted on my taste and love of music. I would find myself humming away, and I remember one of my best friends at school asking me how I knew so many old songs.

So it seemed inevitable that I ended up singing for the choir at school. And from there I progressed to a choir outside of school that began to stage musical productions.

The first show that they put on was a little production of *Oliver!*, and I ended up getting the lead role of Oliver Twist despite never having an acting lesson.

Mum and Dad couldn't believe it when I told them, and I think they were a little bit disbelieving to start with; they probably expected me to be terrible.

But their opinion all changed when they came to watch me on opening night.

I'll never forget my mum's first words to me: 'Oh Hannah, you brought the house down. Oh my God, you were so strong. I can't believe I'm seeing another side of you that I just didn't know existed.'

I think that was because I'd thrown in the towel on the dancing for tennis, and she had never seen me act apart from in my funny little childish holiday performances with Tanya, which lots of kids do.

The buzz from the applause after the show that night was incredible, and all I could think was, I want more of this.

Thankfully, my parents were both impressed enough to agree it was time for some professional singing lessons to explore what they thought might be a little bit of potential from watching me as Oliver.

From there I caught the singing bug. I auditioned for *Annie* at The Marina in Lowestoft and again got the title role.

There were two Annies because her age changes in the

musical, and admittedly the other Annie could sing better, but my sweet mum kindly reckoned I had the audience in the palm of my hand when it came to acting.

Up there, hearing that roaring applause, I didn't want to come off that stage. I just loved it, and Mum and Dad could see how happy it was making me.

The problem was that there wasn't a performing arts school in Great Yarmouth at the time that we knew of, so we didn't know what to do.

It looked like I would just have to carry on with school and choir productions locally and then if I was still interested when I was older, I could try for drama school instead of university.

I was disappointed, but I tried to get on with things at school, hanging out with friends and even sharing my first kiss with a boy from my year at high school called Alex Grimmer – I know, unfortunate name . . .

It took place on the high field at the back of the school. Looking back now it all seems very innocent, but at the time it felt like a little bit of an anti-climax. I'd describe the kiss as a little bit wet and sloppy as we mashed our faces and tongues together. We were kids, finding our way through changing hormones, and neither of us knew what we were doing. I certainly didn't. Does anybody have a perfect first kiss as a teenager?

I don't know why I chose Alex. I don't even think we had a thing for each other, and we only hung out once or twice.

There was a sense of relief that I had ticked that box, but I raced home for dinner straight afterwards and had no desire to repeat the experience any time soon.

Instead I was consumed with landing another musical acting role.

My prayers were answered thanks to lovely Tanya, who came home one day from her travel agent's job with a copy of *The Stage*.

'Here, read this, there's an audition!' she said, slapping the newspaper down on the dining table in front of me while Mum was busy serving up dinner.

The Stage was the holy grail of publications for performers, which had a classified list of upcoming auditions for shows, plays, dances, bands, TV series – everything related to the world of entertainment.

It's where, early in the 90s, five hungry girls answered an ad looking for people to be in a new girl band. Those five ended up being the Spice Girls. But more on them later.

'It's an audition in London for *Annie* with the National Youth Music Theatre, Hannah. You've got to go for it.'

I pleaded to Mum and Dad as they took their seats at the table, 'Please, please Mum, please Dad, will you take me, will you take me to London?'

My parents looked hesitant.

'It's a bit far from here, love, and you are still very young. What about your schoolwork and . . . '

I impatiently cut her off, 'Mum, please, you said I'm a natural at this and have potential, it's all I want to do. Please can I go to London?'

Mum looked at Dad, who nodded, and said, 'Well, all right then. If this is what you really want then we will take you.'

I threw my arms around them and Tanya. 'Thank you, thank you! I won't let you down, I promise.'

Arriving in Islington for the *Annie* audition, I suddenly feel very small.

This was a lot different from the *Annie* audition in Great Yarmouth, and my bravado started to slip.

Groups of young girls full of confidence and sass – like they had all the answers – were lined up in the entrance hall of this great big London school.

I turned to my parents, who gently nudged me forward to receive a number badge before I changed my mind and ran out of the door.

An administrator sticks it on my jumper in a hurry and motions with her hand to go down the corridor and take a seat until my number is called out.

As I get older, I wonder if life is a pre-determined destiny sometimes, or if everything is down to our own luck and what we make for ourselves. I don't suppose we'll ever know anyway!

On that day I believe it was the former, because I was introduced to someone very special who massively shaped my life's direction, even though she or I couldn't possibly have known it then.

Walking slowly along a long, chilly corridor that led to a pair of great big double doors guarding the entrance to my potential future, I hear a sweet voice call out to say there are some seats 'over here'.

I look across and see, sitting by an older lady, a girl of a similar age, hair colouring and build to me, beaming a sunny smile and patting the seat next to her.

It was love at first sight, and I still love her now. My dear friend, Sheridan Smith.

The older lady was Sheridan's mum, who – just like her daughter – was warm, down to earth, friendly and kind.

She instantly put my parents at ease, chatting away to them about how far they had all travelled, while Sheridan and I clicked straight away – nattering like old friends who had known each other our whole lives, so strong was our chemistry.

We were like two peas in a pod, and somehow she made a strange place feel homely and safe.

Sheridan's mum, who was involved in the theatre and music industry, explained to my parents (novices to the whole thing, of course) how it all worked, and seemed to just take me under her wing.

Whatever she said calmed my parents down so much so they went from fretting about the possible dangers of the capital to leaving me with what were two strangers so they could slip off into the city for a wander about on their own.

'She's quite happy playing here with Sheridan. I won't move and will watch over them. Go and do your thing for a few hours,' Sheridan's mum told them.

With that, my mum came across and breezily announced, 'Hannah, your dad and I are going to go out for a bit while you wait here, but we'll be back in two hours – in plenty of time for your audition. Be good for Sheridan's mum, darling.'

I was so entranced by Sheridan, who seemed worldly wise and experienced beyond her years, that I barely noticed my parents walk off.

It was a different story after the audition, which was a disaster. I didn't get a part and bawled my eyes out uncontrollably on poor Sheridan's mum as my parents were still off gallivanting.

As luck would have it, that turned out to be a good thing. Serendipity again in motion, I was left hanging around outside the room as I waited for my parents to return.

The casting director came out saying they were looking for people to try out for a production called *Pendragon*, which told the mythical legend of King Arthur, and called those that were remaining back into the audition room.

I had never heard of *Pendragon*, but with the encouragement of Sheridan's mum, who pointed out it was that or just hanging around the school, off I went with Sheridan to try out.

I had not done any prep, but it wasn't needed. They were teaching us stuff on the day and as it was a new production, nobody would've known any of it anyway.

This meant I relaxed and seemed to pick up the vibe they wanted. All that ad-libbing in the drama cupboard at school – and all my singing and dancing lessons – paid off.

The afternoon grew darker outside as we went through the different stages of dancing, singing, acting, and role play whittling us all down.

In the last stages it ended up being me and one other girl, and we had to battle it out in an argument: whoever shouted the loudest in the verbal sparring match got the part.

So there we were, having this almighty stand-off, shouting louder than foghorns at each other and trying not to laugh at the same time as our voices grew shriller each go.

I'm a lover not a fighter, but somehow I clinched it.

Maybe it was because I was indifferent to *Pendragon*, having so badly had my heart set on playing Annie, that I succeeded; the stakes seemed lower, so the pressure was off.

When I emerged from the audition room, there were Mum and Dad looking panic-stricken.

'Sorry we missed you. You're bright red, darling, what have they had you doing in there?' asked Mum.

I had been working so hard and was full of excitement, which made my face go bright red like a beetroot.

But I didn't care how I looked.

'Mum, Dad, I'm in! I'm in the National Youth Music Theatre. I'm in *Pendragon*. This is it.'

Chapter Three

In the Spotlight

Getting into the National Youth Music Theatre at thirteen felt like a whirlwind and a dream come true.

I never thought I would get in, and it was a shock for my parents to find out I'd only gone and done it by entering a different show that we didn't even know about when we first arrived in London.

We set off back to Great Yarmouth trying to get our heads around it all. And looking back, I imagine it must have been quite a lot for them to take in.

Although I didn't know it immediately at the time, it was a blessing in disguise that I hadn't gotten into *Annie*, because I was to be challenged in learning something completely new and unlike anything I had done before.

Being cast in *Pendragon* was the most magical exhilarating adventure, and it had a massive impact on me.

The National Music Youth Theatre operated in the summer holidays and I found out that *Pendragon* was going to be a travelling production to places such as Hong Kong and New York.

I was so excited because we would be travelling to places I'd never been before.

The furthest I'd travelled in my short time on earth back then was Spain.

Even going down to London was super magical and filled me with excitement, whether it was going with my mum to audition or just shopping at Christmastime. So to be told I was going to be flown to exotic locations around the world was pretty huge to a teenager.

I was so excited, and while Mum and Dad were naturally worried, they agreed to let me go as they knew this was my passion and I was in my element.

Sheridan was in the play too, which made the experience even better, and it put their minds at ease to know I had a friend with me.

In hindsight I'm amazed I wasn't more nervous about travelling far away without my family. I suppose it was teenage bravado. But I was a little nervous about joining the cast, and meeting new people – especially older people.

As you can imagine, there were some loud characters, and a few pretentious, cocky types. But being exposed to that was a money-can't-buy experience; learning how to deal with different people was a great learning curve.

Pendragon was also the show where I first met Paul Cattermole, who had joined the young theatre group with his best mate, Neil.

Paul caught Sheridan's eye first, not mine. When she first clapped eyes on him, she said, 'Oh, he's a hottie!'

I said 'really?' as I was still lusting after Mr Purnell, and teenage boys didn't hold any appeal.

Sheridan liked him as a friend, and the four of us would occasionally hang out, but it never became romantic between any of us. We just had a lot of fun.

The first time performing in *Pendragon* blew me away. The

music and the atmosphere we created with that show was something I'd never experienced.

There was a scene where they'd cover the stage with dry ice and people would become trees. It was ethereal and so magical. And being able to create that, night after night, was a journey I didn't want to end.

The last show we did was on Broadway. It was such a sad moment when the performance finished, and literally everyone was crying – both on stage and in the audience. I will always remember thinking that this was what I wanted to do for the rest of my life, because I always wanted to feel that sense of euphoria I felt on stage.

When it was over, I came back down to earth with a bump and had to go back to school, which was something of a reality check. While I felt very grown up and mature, my friends at school kept me grounded.

Outside of school, I was pushing the boundaries a bit and hanging out with an older crowd; we would go out clubbing in Great Yarmouth. I looked young for my age anyway, so it could be a challenge to get in. But my sister knew the owner of a club called the Ocean Rooms and she used to smuggle me in.

Honestly, I looked ridiculous wearing a little crop top and skirt from the French fashion brand Morgan, which was all the rage at that point in the 90s. It was obvious to everybody in there that I was not eighteen.

I'd tried an alcopop called WKD, and we'd drink tumblers of White Lightning cider until we threw up on the beach.

It felt so illicit and naughty. Around that time, I also tried smoking in an effort to give myself a cool insouciant air, like a French actress. I wanted to like it because I wanted to be cool – as all teenagers dream of – but deep down I wasn't keen on it and thankfully gave up before it became a serious habit.

After *Pendragon* ended I did another summer with the NYMT and stayed until I got into their production of *Bugsy Malone* the following summer. Another dream come true.

My journey towards being a professional actress had begun, but I had some serious decision-making to do. I think you've gathered by now that I wasn't the school swot, but while I was not a screaming academic, I did OK in my GCSEs.

The one subject aside from PE I excelled in was – *surprise surprise* – drama. I received an A* and I think my confidence in the exam and putting on a little play was partly from doing all the shows with the NYMT. I just knew what I was doing when it came to drama studies and so I thought I have to pursue it further.

I told my parents I was moving to London and they were pretty cool about it, considering I was still just sixteen. Sheridan was also moving to London, and so it was decided that we'd share a flat and look after one another. Those next five years with Sheridan were some of the happiest years of my life, and it was then that S Club 7 came calling . . .

Chapter Four

'Do you Know the Way to San Jose?'

I f I thought being in *Pendragon* was an adventure, I had no idea of how my life was going to take off in the most wonderful way.

Shortly after we arrived in the bright city lights of London, both Sheridan and I were cast in *Bugsy Malone*. Sheridan landed the female lead role of Tallulah, in which she shone, and I played gang boss Dandy Dan's wife; the guy who played Dan ended up as my acting agent in later years.

Billy Elliot star Jamie Bell starred in *Bugsy* with us. He played Babyface and he was very memorable as an actor. It's lovely that he's made it in Hollywood and gone on to do some great things. It's quite funny to see him all grown up and playing these very manly, action-hero-type roles. You remember people as the age you found them and when I worked with him he was a tiny boy, five years my junior, so I still think of him as 'Little Jamie' on account that he was so small and very young.

I was sixteen and earning £250 a week, which felt like a king's ransom at the time.

Sheridan and I had a group of friends from the show who wanted to live with us, so we all moved into a flat near

Blackheath in south-east London. It was on the ground floor of a council block on Westcombe Park Road, and it was owned by the father of my *Bugsy Malone* castmate Barnaby.

It was a basic, dinky little two beds, one bath property, but somehow we just made it work having six of us live there. Sheridan and I shared one bedroom and the four boys – Paul Low, Michael Jibson, Matt Fraser and Jeremy Joyce – divided up the second bedroom and lounge between them. We were like sardines in that place, but I didn't care. We were all really close. We were tight. We just got on as a group and had each other's backs. And we've all kept in touch; we still meet up at *Bugsy* reunions and all sorts.

It had a tiny little kitchen. None of us were able to cook apart from Mike, who had this one signature dish he'd serve up nearly every day – sausage pasta. It was as appetising as it sounds. To be fair to Mike, it didn't taste too bad, and it was more than I could muster up; despite my mum being a great cook, I hadn't inherited her culinary skills yet.

And Sheridan definitely couldn't cook, so when Mike wasn't there to feed us, Sheridan and I would go to McDonald's on the way to the theatre for a Sausage McMuffin or a Happy Meal for our dinner.

It was really bad. In between meals we'd live off chocolate and crisps.

Our diet was appalling during that time. I don't think we consumed a single vegetable or piece of fruit in the three months we worked in that show at the Queen's Theatre.

The beds were rock hard but we never felt a tinge of homesickness – even though the phone was a payphone down the other end of the street. No disrespect to home, but we didn't really have the luxury of time for homesickness. Nor did we moan about our flatmates.

Our busy days were filled with laughter and trying to establish ourselves as credible performers and entertainers in the industry. We'd constantly be asking ourselves what was next, and trying to work out where we were going in our careers.

At that age everything is an adventure, and I was so happy to taste freedom and have lots of fun away from home. Plus it meant no longer having to sneak out to clubs behind my parents' backs and hide my hangover on a Sunday.

Considering there were six of us in a two-bedroom flat, I don't remember it being that messy. Paul in particular was extremely neat. He would always have his next day's outfit folded up at the bottom of the bed with his shoes and socks ready to put on. He didn't put up with the other boys being untidy, because they were sharing rooms.

I just don't think we had enough stuff to make a mess. Sheridan and I had turned up with one tiny suitcase each. Crop tops, boob tubes, skirts and shorts. We packed light!

Nevertheless, Sheridan would always leave her clothes everywhere, and she used to borrow my clothes all the time because she'd never have anything clean to wear. We couldn't wash our clothes there, so Sheridan and I would go off to the launderette; when I managed to drag her there it was an adventure in itself. We weren't organised enough to have a set day; on Sundays we'd lie in bed sleeping for hours. It was more a case of as and when.

Down at the launderette, we'd come up with a song and dance routine to entertain ourselves during the wash and dry service. A favourite track to sing was Dionne Warwick's song 'Do You Know the Way to San Jose?' It became our signature song, and we'd belt it out and perform a series of moves to it that I still remember to this day.

The next flat that Sheridan and I moved into together was in Kilburn, North London, and I loved living there with her. Our flat quickly gained a reputation among our theatre troupe as a bit of a liability.

The lot of us were out there in terms of self-discipline, boundaries, general hygiene and living habits, so totally on the same wavelength, or no wavelength really at all.

In Sheridan I felt I had gained another sister. People have commented in the past about a similarity in our appearances, and sometimes I see a picture pop up of her and think it's me.

I loved her from the moment we met, and we gravitated quite intensely towards each other.

The five years we spent living on and off together are some of the happiest, most treasured times of my life.

Even though she is two months younger than me, and Sheridan will probably disagree with me on this, out of the two of us she was the instigator of any naughtiness. She is a strong character – no one can tell Sheridan what to do.

I remember one time when we stayed up in the night playing drinking games, dancing up a storm until we all passed out in the lounge at dawn. The trouble was, that the time we fell asleep was the time Sheridan and some of the others should have been getting showered and ready because they were meant to be going on the TV show *This Morning* to promote *Bugsy Malone*.

Instead, I woke up with a tongue like fur and switched

on the telly to hear the music from *This Morning* cheerily ringing out.

As I stared gormlessly at the screen, trying to focus while the others were still snoring away, somewhere in the hungover recesses of my mind was a voice telling me that they had an important meeting with the programme.

But with my brain not running at full capacity, I simply shrugged it off as dehydration-induced delirium and dragged myself off the sofa in search of some Diet Coke to quench my raging thirst.

Sheridan woke up with a start, groaning at my clattering about the apartment and looking as terrible as I felt.

Holding her head in her hands she whimpered, 'Has anyone got any painkillers?'

She lifted her head up to look at the TV screen and her eyes widened in horror.

'Fuck!' she yelled. 'What's the time? We need to be on telly at 10.30!'

The lads jumped awake in shock at Sheridan's foghorn alarm call.

All of us had been in such a deep sleep that no one had heard the flat bell ringing earlier that morning. The programme makers of This Morning had sent a driver and car to take them to the studio but failing to rouse everyone from our slumber, they'd given up and cleared off.

'I think you're a bit late for that,' I laughed and passed out in my bed.

God, everyone was so naughty at times, but that's what being a teenager is about.

Nevertheless, even though we were super young, excited

and probably all over the place, there was a level of discipline there – otherwise we wouldn't have been able to do the job.

We did however carry our reputation with us from that house to mine and Sheridan's next flat share, where some of Sheridan's friends would drop in, including Sid Owen and Dean Gaffney off *EastEnders*. Sid used to love to sing and when the four of us were together and drunk he'd get on the piano and rattle out the tunes. It was hilarious watching him go for it, as up till that point I'd known him as 'Rickkkkkkky!'

Dean Gaffney was a great lad and we loved going out clubbing in London together and hitting the dance floor. Dean received a certain amount of admiration from the young ladies at that time, who all seemed to love him. But we were just mates, and he used to come back to the flat quite a lot after a night out dancing at Chinawhite or Purple.

Another welcome visitor was Ritchie from Five, who had come round to see Sheridan. That was quite a funny night, pretty sure we talked nonsense into the early hours.

Andrew-Lee Potts – one of Sheridan's friends – came back to the flat at one point, disappearing during the night and turning up later randomly with an orange juice because I'd told him I liked orange juice.

Being the tallest and slightly older-looking, our flatmates Mike and Matt would be sent down to the local off-licence to try and buy booze, and the nights we struck lucky meant party time.

We loved to play pranks on each other. I remember we made a fake spliff and gave it to one of the housemates to smoke. I will spare his blushes and not name him, but he acted like he was stoned off his head after a few drags, giggling his head off and going along with the motions as though he'd smoked the strongest doobie; the placebo effect was strong. I know it was unfair but we were killing ourselves laughing at him acting off his face. We couldn't bear to tell him that the spliff had no cannabis resin in it because his embarrassment would have been off the scale.

At night, Sheridan and I would lie awake in our beds nattering into the early hours about which boys we fancied in the cast and other silly stuff. We often talked about my crush on our flatmate Jeremy, and I used to ask Sheridan if she thought he fancied me too.

One night, after a little drink, I shared a cheeky kiss with Jeremy. It was very innocent, and bless us, we ended up getting together.

When we left the show we would write to each other, which is quite sweet, looking back, because nobody does that anymore – we just don't do love letters, do we?

Hollywood was certainly a million miles away from our former council flat in south-east London, so our romantic notions were much closer to home. Literally.

Sheridan may also have kissed one of the boys too during that time period, but she was so busy with her role in the play, and it didn't leave her much time for romance.

She did play Cupid between me and another one of her friends, who I later went out with. He had come over once to the flat and I'd spoken to her a lot about liking him, so she probably helped sort of manifest it because we were both too shy to make a move. But that's for another chapter.

The reality is that doing eight shows a week meant that there wasn't much downtime, and we'd often need to be in early for rehearsals and stuff like that to make changes to the show.

So despite some of our antics outside of work, there was a lot of structure within the chaos and we never missed a live theatre show.

Sheridan and I both realised during this exciting period, that it would be very difficult to go back home to our humdrum lives now. In our last month of *Bugsy*, we started planning and scheming how we could stay in London after the show ended.

Sometimes your prayers are answered and my angel saviour appeared again in the form of Sheridan's mum, who is just the cutest, most gorgeous person.

Sheridan had been outside the flat for ages, in the big red phone box chatting to her mum.

When she walked back into the flat, she seemed excited and eager to talk to me.

'Hannah, Mum's just told me an advert has gone out in *The Stage* for an audition tomorrow in town, looking for pop stars. They might be looking to create another band like the Spice Girls. Look, we've both got the day off tomorrow, and we can't go over to the pub because they'll chuck us out without the others. Come on, neither of us look eighteen. Let's do something a bit different. It's bound to be terrible, so shall we just go along to have a laugh and see what everyone is wearing?'

Sheridan always knew how to make even the most innocuous of events sound interesting.

I said, 'Yeah, yeah, OK then. I'm up for that.'

Sheridan looked delighted and dragged me up off the sofa.

'Come on, we'll need to plan our outfits. This is going to be wild.'

She raced to the bedroom to try on clothes.

Now, being in a pop band held no interest or appeal to me. But when that audition came through, one reason I said yes to going was that subconsciously I realised if it were to work out and we got selected, we wouldn't have to go back to normal life.

I followed Sheridan into the bedroom and began tearing out clothes from my case to see what crazy looks I could conjure up.

With our first pay cheque from *Bugsy*, the first thing Sheridan and I had bought was a pair of Buffalo shoes each. Rent was £50 each so we had £200 with which to splurge.

Back in 1997, when the Spice Girls were dominating the pop scene, Buffalo shoes were the things to be seen in.

So,with that first salary in our new current accounts, we raced off together to a shoe shop in Neal Street, Covent Garden, where I paid £80 for a khaki-coloured pair of Buffalos with black soles.

I absolutely loved those shoes. Taking them out the box and waving them at her, I said, 'Sheridan, we have to wear our Buffalos tomorrow'.

She was moving around in front of the mirror holding two different skirts up against her waist and asked 'which one?'

That night we had a riot playing dress up for that audition and choosing our hairstyles; we weren't taking the audition seriously at that point.

That evening I trooped outside to call Mum from the red phone box and fill her in on our plans. She sounded horrified when I said the audition was not for a new stage or TV show but a pop group.

'Oh no, Hannah, why a band? You're doing so well with your acting. It sounds interesting, but this doesn't sound like the right audition for you. I am not sure why even Sheridan is bothering. It will be filled with young ladies trying to look like another version of the Spice Girls. Don't waste your time on it.'

I tried to reassure her, 'Mum it's not me. Sheridan is doing the audition. I'm just going to keep her company. I agree it sounds terrible. We've got the day off and I will go along to have a laugh and just to see what it's all about. There's no harm in it.'

Mum asked what Sheridan's mother thought about it all.

When I told her she was the one who'd spotted the ad, Mum was a bit more amenable and said 'OK then, have fun.' I put the receiver down.

If I'm being honest, I found the whole premise of me being in a pop band preposterous, and never thought it would be anything to worry about.

But sometimes the universe has other plans.

Chapter Five

Reach for the Stars

S heridan and I sprang out of bed the morning of the audition full of excitement in a race to be first to the bathroom.

She won. As she seemed more keen about the whole thing, I played it casually and decided not to put my hair in little Baby Spice-style bunches as I'd planned to, and just to leave it hanging loose.

I wore a denim jacket, cropped T-shirt, combats and my khaki-green Buffalos.

Sheridan emerged looking amazing in her denim skirt and Buffalos.

We were absolutely buzzing when we set off towards Pineapple Dance Studios.

At the time we just had this confidence together, which was ridiculous; it was probably *over*confidence. But we were absolutely buzzing with excitement and laughing our heads off.

When we rocked up to the venue there were loads of people and a long queue snaked out the door, going round and round past the building and around the block. It was mostly girls wearing Buffalos on their feet like us.

My zeal started to wane and seeing the dismay on my face, Sheridan hooked my arm with hers and tried to buoy me back up with a friendly pep talk.

'Come on, Hannah, remember why we're here. It will be a laugh, so we may as well wait in the line and give it a go – it is moving quite quickly.'

We joined what was like a conveyor belt of other young women, repeatedly shuffling forward a few metres and stopping again.

As we got closer to the audition room, I vividly remember seeing Bradley through a window, looking like he was having his own private audition, dancing and singing away. Watching him, Sheridan and I were really impressed and we wondered who this man was and why he was having a private audition. He seemed to be having the time of his life there – he was full of energy and very polished.

To be fair to Bradley, he looked like a ready-made pop star with this air of cocky confidence that seemed to have quite an effect on women – so much so that when he walked out the room smiling, lots of the girls waiting in the line were enamoured by his presence. They started fangirling him, touching his bum and tapping him as he came past like he was already a big star.

We watched on with bemusement as he lapped up the attention with a cheeky smile on his face.

'Did you see that? Is that guy famous? Who is he?' I asked Sheridan.

But it wouldn't be long before I found out. I couldn't possibly have known that this handsome young stranger would go on to be a sizeable part of my future career.

As I looked around, I could see this audition meant such a lot to people, like the *Annie* casting had for me.

Sheridan was calm and cheery, and seemed to be taking it all in her stride.

She's probably done loads of these, I thought to myself. I bet she sails through this.

At that point a young man called out 'this way please' and beckoned us and around forty others to follow him through the double doors into a large room.

They ushered a load of people through until you couldn't get any more in the room and then we were divided into two lines of about twenty people each.

I noticed four faceless people standing at the back of the room, watching us.

Sheridan was in a different line to me but I gave her a quick good luck and she grinned back at me.

It was cut-throat in that place, and there was no time for any nerves or fear – you had to just roll with it.

Both the lines learned a short dance routine with Sheridan's group going up first to perform.

They did their thing and after the dance a faceless person walked towards the group and selected the people that would be going through to the next round.

To my total shock, his finger missed Sheridan.

'The rest of you, thanks for coming but that will be all for today – you'll not be required to stay. The others who haven't yet danced, please get ready to perform the routine next.'

If she was disappointed to not have been chosen, then Sheridan – who is always a consummate professional – never showed it.

I did though, and mouthed to her, 'What the fuck are they doing? Like what the fuck is happening right now?'

She gave me one of her beautiful big smiles and said, 'Good luck, Hannah, go for it.' And with that she grabbed her bag and left me.

I was absolutely gobsmacked that Sheridan hadn't been chosen to stay and just felt so bad at the time, thinking, *Oh my God, this girl is so much better than me.*

It felt unfair that Sheridan, with her amazing voice, wasn't put through and given the chance to sing when she would have blown the entire room away. I just couldn't believe that; it felt completely wrong.

On their command, when it was our line's turn I went through the motions as asked, my mind still whirring from the shock of them not choosing Sheridan.

At the end I expected them to kick me out and was ready to go and join Sheridan to laugh about it and treat ourselves to a McDonald's on the way home.

But to my even greater surprise, they didn't reject me.

Our group was sliced down, again from twenty to ten, and those of us remaining were asked to sing our chosen pieces before the next load of people came through the door.

I had picked this song I loved from the Disney film *Pocahontas*, which had been released two years before.

In my head I sounded terrible. Singing was never my strong point!

That's why it always makes me laugh. I remember thinking, I'm going to really go for this because I know four lines of the song really well – I used to love singing that little section. And thankfully, that's all they needed. It wasn't like they wanted a full-blown version of the whole song anyway. Then I would have been fucked.

But for what felt like some random reason, at the end of it they said to me, OK, *you're still in the running.*

I felt elation mixed with incredulity. Although I still wasn't fully au fait with what they were looking for. I knew they were planning a new band, but that was it. Looking around at the others remaining in the room I didn't see anybody at this point who would be joining me later. Bradley was the only person I saw that day who would be in the group, but I wasn't to know that then.

All I know is that one of the faceless people politely said to me, 'Thanks, leave your details and we will be in touch about the next part'. The funny thing is, I had to give them my parents' number and address because I could hardly give them the number of a public phone box, could I?

Gosh, my mum's not going to believe this, I thought when I emerged into the early evening.

What a day, what an experience.

Sheridan had long since gone home, and so when I arrived back on our road I went straight to the phone box to call Mum and Dad and tell them before going into the flat.

They were as shocked and as surprised as me at the news.

Mum was like, 'Pardon, Hannah? I don't understand. You've never wanted to be in a pop band? You said you were just going to support Sheridan and that it was all a bit of a laugh.' I responded silently by nodding my head.

'I can't believe they didn't take Sheridan,' she continued. 'She was the one who wanted to go and she's so talented. But I know they just go on looks to be begin with because it sounds like this fella is trying to do a younger version of the Spice Girls. I hope she's OK and doesn't take it to heart.'

Dad was in the background, firing off questions through Mum, who was hogging the phone.

I was like, 'Mum, tell Dad I really didn't think this would happen. I told you both it was just a fun thing, but they want me back to audition again. I'm as surprised as you guys are, but I may as well try and see where it takes me until I land a good acting role,' I continued, trying to convince myself as much as them that I had a future in the record industry.

'By the way, they will call you tomorrow at some point to tell you what I have to do next so please take down all the details they give you and I will ring you tomorrow afternoon to find out.'

Mum sighed, 'OK, well I just can't believe it. Well done, Hannah. What are you going to wear for the next one? Maybe wear your hair like Baby Spice does . . . '

I started to yawn.

'Mum, I love you and I'm tired, call you tomorrow.'

As I put the receiver down, I could hear her telling me, 'Please get some sleep'.

Walking back to the flat, I thought about what my mother had said about the band being chosen on looks.

They hadn't actually said that they wanted to create a new Spice Girls, but thinking back to the audition I did seem to be the only blonde-haired girl in the room that had been chosen for round two.

When I got back inside our flat, Sheridan was waiting to give me the biggest hug. She wasn't affected by the audition knock-back in the slightest.

I think we can all see and agree that given her well-deserved success and critical acclaim as one of our best ever and most-loved actresses, she's got the right thing going on today!

So not getting into the band didn't faze her in the least, even though she had instigated going for it. We had a good giggle about it – she laughed her head off – but she did say, 'Hannah, you need to go for this. This could be really good for you'.

I felt very conflicted about this new career path in music that had opened up in front of me. It wasn't something that I had planned for or even considered before. I hadn't set out to be part of a pop group. I didn't dream at night of selling out stadiums or having a number-one record.

I wasn't even hugely drawn towards the whole pop scene.

Yes, I had fun belting out a Spice Girls number in the flat with Sheridan now and again, but I *loved* singing the songs from musicals, and the other old-school stuff I had been brought up on.

It was as though this thing bigger than me had happened, and I wasn't in control of my destiny at that point. Like in *The Truman Show*, there was some unseen force orchestrating my life for me.

There was also the fact that it would've been amazing if the both of us had gotten in. The idea of us being in the band together was much more appealing than doing it by myself. We could have been the new Emma and Geri, we joked.

So, when Sheridan was fast asleep, I was left reeling by the day's unexpected turn of events, trying to get my head around what had happened.

Unable to sleep, I lay there thinking, *God, is being a pop singer even what I want to do?*

Up until that moment I had been sort of finding my way in the theatre and entertainment industry. I saw myself as a jobbing actress going up for auditions rather than a pop star, and thought I would continue what I set out to do originally – act.

Besides, I intended to do it all with my best mate by my side – because whatever we stepped into, we found a funny way of dealing with it and made it exciting. So the concept of joining a band without her made me uncomfortable. I was conflicted and couldn't decide if I should continue on this journey.

Nevertheless, Sheridan herself was not personally affected in the slightest. Her family are in the theatre world, and she'd done a lot already at this point. Her future was secured and without doubt going to be super bright – that I felt certain of.

Above all, this was more than a moment. It was huge in terms of my life path.

During my time at the National Youth Music Theatre, I learned a lot about what I was good and not good at. I had noticed that I wasn't getting picked for the big singing roles as much as I was cast for my acting. For this reason I didn't have that innate confidence of knowing I'd been born with this amazing voice – I didn't think, *This is what I want to do and I'm going to nail it.*

It was a journey, or a process of discovery. Notably I'd hit a point, probably around the age of fifteen, when I thought there wasn't much sense in pursuing singing. Prior to that I was possibly still hoping my singing would come through somehow. I had become slightly disheartened around that time, as it didn't seem like it was ever going to happen for me.

My burning ambition to be in *Rent* seemed as out of reach as having a number one single.

Sometimes when you push so hard for something, and really want something to happen, it just doesn't. But they say when you aren't pushing for something is usually when it happens.

It was strange, like being on a fairground ride that I couldn't step off because it was too exciting and I just had to see where it went. But at the same time I was obviously not in control of where it was going.

I think sometimes in life we hit a crossroads and we don't know which direction to take.

It's the thought that if we take the wrong turn, will we miss out on an amazing opportunity someplace further down the road?

I like to think what is meant for us won't pass us by if we don't jump at every chance. But, I've gone through periods in my life where I have tried to push harder and not surrender in a bid to make something happen rather than just let what's meant for me, be.

I've also come up against obstacles more by pushing for things too hard, so for me personally, it's been about trying to get that balance in terms of allowing life to happen, but not sitting back too much.

I wasn't sitting back even then, but I think as you get older you realise that things will never be perfect and you can always make something of the situation, whatever it is.

We constantly experience *Sliding Doors* moments, when if

you had missed the train at the platform your life would take a different turn.

With that going around in my head, I blocked out what was expected of me and made my mind up to go for it and get on the proverbial train.

Getting into the band was a very lengthy, drawn-out and intense process that took around seven months in total.

I attended a second audition at another London dance centre with people I hadn't seen at the first round.

This time I prepared a couple of songs and took it more seriously than I had the first.

It was tougher in terms of the routines we were learning and performing, and I felt the pressure. They kept switching people in and out of small groups until the end of the day when a lovely man called Nick Godwin, who was involved in the selection process and was later to be the band's manager, came over to see me. He had been sat down on a chair in the corner of the room and he just had this warm demeanour. He asked me to join him for a one-on-one chat in which he took the time to listen to me and find out what my journey was and how I had got into that room. It felt a lot more personable then the first audition. So personable in fact that his mother turned out to be my parents' neighbour!

He explained they were looking to put together a co-ed – a mixed-gender band – with no definite specifics of how many girls or boys. They thought the band would likely have about five members but they'd see as we went along and at that stage they didn't really know for sure how many people they wanted.

I also had no idea that the TV show was going to be involved during the early days, but to a teenage girl it sounded a lot of fun: there would be rehearsals for the band, just as there would be for a play.

After this warm, encouraging conversation with Nick, it was beginning to feel like, blimey, this is something that might actually happen for me.

I understood that I was being put through because I must have had a look they wanted and I got the smallest glimmer of hope that I was in with a good chance.

And it just went on from there.

By this point, *Bugsy* was over and it was time to say a temporary goodbye to Sheridan.

It was a very dramatic farewell when I moved back to my parents' house in Norfolk. We cried and promised to write letters, which I did, to keep her up to date with what was happening with the band. But it wouldn't be that long until I was back living with her – in her I knew I had a best friend for life.

As they were trialling different people over the coming months, the first band member I met was Tina Barrett, who had been talent-spotted and invited to try out for the band.

Tina was doing these sort of dance/modelling jobs where she'd sashay along the catwalk and then do maybe eight beats of a dance at the end, and my first thought on seeing her was, *What great legs*. I remember going to see one of her dance/model shows and she had this cool black bob. I loved her look.

Getting along was really, really important for management – the key thing – and we were trialled in terms of getting along with each other.

So, the first people that were put together, that I knew of, were me, Tina and Paul, who I knew from three years earlier when we'd acted together in *Pendragon*.

Obviously that was surreal in itself, because I knew him extremely well. I remember the first time when we met on the S Club circuit, it was a case of 'What are you doing here? Are you actually here as part of the thing?' I mean, we knew we both had to be, but still felt an is-this-really-happening kind of vibe, but we laughed together afterwards.

Then they'd be looking for the next band member and then they would bring in another person, and so on and so on.

The management company asked us if we'd start hanging out together and various people were brought in and out over the course of the next few months.

Tina was the oldest. She had a little one-bed flat in Hammersmith with a cat, and we'd go over to hers and eat together or sometimes I'd sleep over so I didn't have to travel back to my parents.

With the cost of driving up and down in my little Peugeot 205, it made more sense to move down and get a flat.

Tina's one-bed was not big enough for me to move into, so having known Paul from the National Youth Music Theatre for three years I suggested that he and I rent a couple of rooms together.

We went flat hunting together, and circling the places in the paper you were going to ring was quite fun. In some ways – before we moved fully to the internet – it was more straightforward doing it that way.

There was a lot of trial and error along the road to forming the band. There was one girl we saw a lot of at that point who didn't make it through, and they had talent scouts out looking for people.

I remember Paul, Tina and I meeting a young girl who was just fourteen. She sounded incredible on demos in the studio, but she was too young and wasn't quite ready to be living away from home, so they decided that it was too early for her. And so she just went back to school.

I didn't see Rachel at any of the public auditions I attended. Her brother was working at a record company and she went in to see him for lunch or something like that where she was spotted. Which you wouldn't find too surprising!

The first time we were introduced I remember being mesmerised by her amazing hair. I don't think it moved. And of course, Rachel has a very distinctive look, which proved to be a huge hit!

There was this other girl, also called Hannah, who was older than me. She was unbelievably striking to look at, with a cloud of beautiful red hair and pale skin, and she was a really good dancer. She was beautiful, and at the time was studying acting at the famous Mountview drama school.

Being more mature than the rest of us, she decided to pull out and told a disappointed management, 'I don't think I'm right for this. But I know somebody who is.'

Hence we met her friend Paul, who I already knew and hadn't seen since Pendragon. I believe management then went to see Paul in action at a show – and then the rest, as they say, is history.

Bradley slipped in and naturally I recognised him from the first audition, where he had been fast tracked, and told him, 'I remember I saw you strutting your stuff through the window'.

He laughed and we had a giggle over it; he slotted in really well with everybody.

So we were definitely going to be more than a five. I think it was then decided that they wanted a big gang, and we needed a strong female vocal lead, which would take the band to seven people.

Last but not least, there was larger-than-life Jo, who had previously been in a band. Jo was different from anyone that I had met before. There was no one really like her where I grew up, and I still hadn't really come across anybody who was a proper Essex girl. She was just this big character in her own right, and was authentically herself.

It was then that I had the realisation that this was all real and I would be knocking the acting auditions on the head.

The band was formed of really different people, but we all gelled well and everyone got on from the moment we started recording.

Some were closer than others, as naturally happens. I had a particularly strong bond with Tina and Paul, having been placed with them from the beginning, and I adored Bradley.

Tina, even though she was bombshell sexy, was inclined to roll her eyes at the same things I did, as girls do. She and I were on a similar wavelength.

Jo and Rachel were initially very close. (Just as mates. There were no girl-on-girl romances in our band.) We all shared beds, but strictly platonically, so if you're looking for a Mel B and Geri-style scandal, I am sorry to disappoint.

That would be a story, wouldn't it?

But the beauty of it was all these personalities complementing one another because we probably wouldn't really have chosen each other as friends in real life; in terms of the band, it had to be that way, and it just worked.

There was a synergy to us that felt good. We were S Club 7 – our own family for the next five years.

Chapter Six

Full Disclosure

The band's creation was the brainchild of Simon Fuller – a music mogul and British entrepreneur.

By 1998 Fuller had achieved fame and mammoth success for masterminding the Spice Girls and he would go on to create the commercially successful TV franchise *Pop Idol*.

He was a serious figure who, whenever he entered a room, commanded respect without saying anything. He didn't have to court publicity or make his presence known, because when he spoke, people in the industry listened and did as they were told.

There was no doubt, given his ability to spot a gap in the entertainment market, that if Simon put his hand to something it would turn to gold. He certainly had the Midas Touch.

I had briefly seen him during audition three, but it was around the time of the fourth audition when I was formally introduced to Simon at a celebratory meeting in his house in Richmond.

My first impressions were that he was very polite, reserved and gentle. He spoke softly, there were no raised voices or swearing, and I noticed that he would take his time when answering a question. I've been asked if I was frightened of him and I would not go as far as saying that, but I instinctively knew that this was a man I didn't want to get on the wrong side of.

He was just naturally a powerful force and I don't think anybody would wilfully cross him.

And he always dressed very plainly. Like he was wearing a uniform: a simple shirt and trousers. It almost felt like he wore the same outfit all the time, and you could imagine that he'd found a shirt that he really liked and had about a hundred of them in his wardrobe.

There wasn't a family atmosphere in his house when I walked in back then. Not that I could tell. And I knew nothing of his marital status at that stage but it feels odd to think he was younger than I am now when he was in that position. He just was one of those people who seemed older than their years. Incredibly bright, driven, sharp and well read.

The house was not modern at all, rather the sort of home you'd imagine belonging to a posh older gentleman. It contained beautiful old paintings, and I don't think any of us had seen quite such a luxurious house before; we were all probably a bit overawed and wowed.

We were led through to his lounge and we politely chatted about our day and how we were feeling. We sat down with a glass of water each, and he went around the group and asked us, one at a time, to give two characteristics to describe ourselves.

It felt a bit random at the time, but now I realise that was obviously for the TV show and he was trying to evaluate our personalities to create our individual characters, just as the Spice Girls were known as Posh, Baby, Ginger, Scary and Sporty.

I think I said something daft along the lines of 'I'm cheeky and fun!' with a giggle.

He gave me an unimpressed look and turned his head to look at Jo. I sank back and thought, Oh no, should I have said something else?

I don't remember exactly what Jo said. Maybe something along the lines of 'loud and feisty', and whatever Rachel said, they probably put her down as the 'sexy one'. Bradley was perceived to be the 'ladies' man', and Jon, the biggest joker out of all of us. Tina may have mentioned dancing, as she certainly had the best moves out of all of us and strangely I don't seem to remember what Paul said.

But you got the vibe that he knew already that he had found what he had been looking for.

Then we were invited to his villa in southern Italy.

It was austere, just a piano in an otherwise barely furnished room: nothing like his Richmond house.

It was very much like a single man's pad, which looked impressive but didn't feel warm or welcoming.

But Simon was determined to show us the time of our lives.

Even though we had not signed any contracts, I remember having a chat about what being in the band was really going to entail.

He told us the name would be S Club 7 – we suspected that the S stood for Simon and we were to be the seven.

We gasped and all looked around at each other with excited faces. I guess that confirmed that we were in the band – yes!

And it was then my ears really pricked up, because he dropped the bomb on us that there was to be a TV series.

Acting! I can't speak for other members of the band at that moment, but *I* was excited by the prospect of doing a TV show.

Then the best part was we would be going out to America to film it. I think that really stoked the fire, and I was buzzing. It was just something I hadn't expected; I felt like this was my big break now and that this was meant to be.

We were all elated and he put on a couple of demo tracks for us. None of us had seen a contract yet but it was now confirmed by the man himself that we were in.

During that trip he took us all to the island of Capri for shopping. It was so very glamorous. We were allowed to choose any item we wanted.

The prices of clothes there were probably more than I'd paid for my Peugeot, and I did feel overwhelmed by it all. There we were, a bunch of kids, wandering around the extremely charming streets of Capri popping into loads of different luxury designer shops like Prada to see if anything took our fancy. It was like *Pretty Woman*, when Richard Gere's character takes Julia Roberts shopping on Rodeo Drive. And we probably looked like Julia the first time she walked in!

The girls almost squealed in excitement. It was like being let out of school almost to run amok and he sort of hung about in the background watching us wander around the shops and then he would pop over and say, 'Have you found something then?'

I think Rachel, who seemed the most confident of us in

that situation, like a natural, picked out a dress, and the lads chose tops and sunglasses from various places, while I didn't have a clue and just selected a small bag because it looked neat and dinky. Why didn't I choose a Rolex lol?! I didn't ask how much it was. I was much too embarrassed to check in front of him, but Simon just smiled benignly and asked the assistant to wrap it, maybe 'cos I didn't choose the Rolex! I imagine he used that shopping day as a way to suss us all out and assess our personalities to see how we interacted with each other, with strangers, and also how we were around him, which was pretty magnetic, I suppose as he was the main man, the Big Cheese, the Guvna!

Our weekend of scheduled indulgence continued. That night he had a private chef come to the villa to cook our dinner, and he presented each of us with a personal gift.

It was a Tiffany choker necklace wrapped up inside the famous blue Tiffany's giftbag. It was really chunky with a heart, and clearly expensive, albeit not something I would pick for myself.

The other girls gasped in joy when they saw it was from Tiffany's, so I put my most thrilled expression on my face and said thank you.

He seemed pleased by my reaction and it was indeed a very generous gift.

Another thing that I remember him doing was having gold cards made for us. Sadly they were not gold Amexes – that would be a step too far in the hands of a bunch of teenagers – but he presented us with these gold-wrapped boxes, inside each of which was an unusable gold card.

They were printed with our name and a run of numbers

from one to seven written on them, and they said we belonged to S Club 7.

I suppose they were a unique personalised membership card to a special club of his, so to speak.

It's a shame but I haven't got mine anymore. I must have lost it during my last move.

Looking back, I think Simon was quite sentimental with the whole gold card thing; he had put thought into it.

He was giving us a taste of an elite world – the kind of life being rich affords you – top restaurants, flash clothes, holidays and cars.

By taking us on this trip, giving us these gifts, he was dangling the prospect of luxury: if you work hard you will be granted this lifestyle and power like mine.

It felt tantalising to be allowed in to try it. It was a heady, intoxicating mix

When we got back to London, there'd be very lovely cars taking us everywhere. After having to take tubes and buses, all of a sudden we'd be picked up in a SUV and have a driver. We were very quickly getting used to that luxury lifestyle. It was wonderful at the time but probably not a healthy habit to form at sixteen in hindsight ... I may still be prone to indulging myself in a bit of unnecessary and overpriced luxury now and again, so dare I say it's become a hard habit to kick!

After we released new music, Simon would always be the person to come in and give the good news and inform us of what he had planned next for the band and the show.

We didn't deal with Simon on a day-to-day basis and had little contact throughout the five years we were together; if there was a tough situation going on or something that we needed to talk about, he had a team for that.

During my time in the band my life was essentially signed over to 19 Entertainment: there were no sick days or compassionate leave. This sounds a lot worse than it was as I didn't really need any compassionate leave and was rarely sick, but knowing it's not an option does carry with it quite a large amount of pressure. Given the dynamic of seven people being in perfect order the entire time, it seems somewhat miraculous we were as consistent as we were. I couldn't even maintain that level of work for a week now, I wouldn't think. I'd love to though, at least be able to, and there's me moaning about it in the previous sentence!

As a youngster, I was an incubus for germs and would come down with flu most winters.

S Club did have Christmas off, and then of course, the adrenaline stops – boom! – I succumbed to the plague.

My temperature was sky high and I was delirious from the sweats. Mum was extremely worried and rang them on Boxing Day evening to say I couldn't come back to London the next day as I was extremely poorly and the doctor said I needed a full week of bed rest.

Management made it clear in no uncertain terms that I had to be back or else.

She realised that she no longer had me in her care, and while under that contract I didn't belong to her.

They could lay the law down like that.

Of course, my parents met with Simon and 19 Entertainment and all the other parents in 1998.

Management were all so charming and my parents were

excited, thinking this was a great opportunity for them and us.

My parents tell me they were kept at arm's length, and that when they spoke to the other mums and dads, they all reassured themselves that this was a wonderful opportunity.

Especially when they said that there was going to be a TV series. Mum said, 'Oh, at least Hannah's getting back to acting again.'

But she only realised later that it wasn't the acting that she had hoped I would be doing. I don't think I really developed as an actress within those five years, and Mum says she regrets letting me do it.

She tells me, 'I think everything was taken out of our control as soon as you signed up for it, and we couldn't have any control over anything. I suppose when you're younger, all you want to do is be on stage, that's all the fun side of it. But people will jump at chances of course. Because they think fame is the best thing to happen to them – being on TV, being on the stage. And they'll do anything to get it.'

Chapter Seven

Welcome to Miami!

Obliviously I don't remember this moment because I was 13 months old, but it is my favourite picture of me and my mum.

Tucking into a holiday treat with my dad in Spain.

Having a blast in my bin liner witch costume for Halloween.

I have a lot of happy memories of this house in Great Yarmouth and I loved my space-hopper!

Christmas with Stuart and Tanya. You can tell it's the 80s – look at that couch!

Aged 4, on holiday in Spain.

We are elephants, in case you couldn't guess . . .

Aged 7, in full 80s swing!

My leg had come out of a cast, just in time for our local dance show.

Showtime! The *Annie* cast during the 'I Think I'm Gonna Like it Here' number.

Me as Annie, centre stage during 'It's a Hard Knock Life'.

Two Annies with their Daddy Warbucks.

NATIONAL YOUTH MUSIC THEATRE
— Supported by —
SIR ANDREW LLOYD WEBBER

Pendragon

Actor

Hannah Spearritt

My National Youth Music Theatre (NYMT)
card. It was super excited that finally receive
this card and have kept it all these years.

Our final night on *Pendragon* in NYC.
As you can see, we were very emotional
about the show coming to an end.

Playing young Guinevere
in *Pendragon*, my first
production with National
Youth Music Theatre.

On stage during
Act II of *Pendragon*.

Me and Sheridan backstage in our dressing room, Shaftsbury Avenue.

Bugsy Malone, Queen's Theatre, West End. I was 16 years old here.

My on-stage husband (and future agent) mid-performance in *Bugsy*.

Backstage at *Bugsy* with Tallulah and her dancers.

It was always fun letting our hair down after the show.

The gang after the show.

Some of the *Bugsy* cast outside outside our flat in Westbourne Park.

The first few months in the band were exhilarating and a whir of activity as we launched onto the music landscape.

Everything felt new and exciting: being plunged into a studio recording our first album, releasing our first songs, giving radio and TV interviews, speaking to journalists, and all while navigating this journey from unknown to pop star.

My feet didn't touch the floor most days, and I didn't have time to breathe, let alone think deeply about things.

We worked really, really hard and there was no time for any negativity either.

Every day I'd wake up excited about what we would be doing and where we would be going.

The great thing about being in a seven-piece is that you can turn up to work and essentially not do anything. If you're having an off day, you can hang back a little bit and let other people take centre stage and there was huge trust among us.

In the first year of finding our places, there was never really a hierarchy as such.

All of my bandmates sang very well, but we had different types of vocals tonally.

So everyone felt very confident within their voice and that

they had a right to be there; we also all looked quite different from each other.

The boys would naturally gravitate to the back and the girls to the front in videos or when performing on stage. I've never had a discussion with the boys about it, but l think they got enough attention for what they needed, if that's what they were there for. But I don't really think it *was* what they were there for really.

For the girls it almost felt as if we had an extra bit of work to do, because the attention was on us a bit more, and we had a few more photoshoots to do.

The lads were never jealous of that, and were probably just pleased to have the extra time off. I never heard any of them demand to be the cover star of *Attitude* or any of the lads' mags.

The press were quick to paint Rachel as the sexy one and I don't know how she felt about it. I never wanted to be that; I was so young, I didn't really think about putting on a sexy outfit.

I was quite a tomboy character at that point, so sexiness just wasn't my thing. I hated the silver Bacofoil tops they put us in. And those awful belly tops everyone wore at the time.

Obviously I became aware of my body and my appearance through the S Club 7 journey because of all the naked bikini photo shoots.

But not at the beginning. I felt nothing but happiness for Rachel if she was happy about being labelled that way, and relief that I could be myself.

I was very close with all of them back then, in different

ways. I never got a feeling of jealousy among the women, and I doubt Rachel would say anything about the level of coverage she got over the rest of us.

The memories are pretty mad from all that time.

When 'Bring It All Back' reached number one, it was one of the most surreal moments of my entire life. I remember it as freshly as if it were yesterday.

We had been away filming in America when the first TV series, Miami 7, came out in the UK, and by the time we got home there was an audience who loved the theme tune – which was 'Bring It All Back'.

The song had been hammered down people's throats every week on CBBC, because in those days you would come back home after school and probably put on a channel that was a choice of one of five! It's mad to think how much has changed in terms of TV-viewing technology in the twenty-five years since then.

Of course, BBC One was one of those five and that show was on at ten past five every Thursday for thirteen weeks.

So yeah, 'Bring It All Back' went mental when it actually went on sale; young people and probably their parents too had seized on it, which was completely nuts, but it was amazing, obviously, to have so many fans love the music you are producing for them.

We were performing at Party in the Park that summer in front of an audience of 100,000 people – our first really big gig – and it was announced live on stage that the song was number one. It was such a huge moment that is quite incredible to comprehend.

Although it had been figured out by management this was

going to be big thanks to the TV show, as a band we never really knew what was happening or going to happen.

It wasn't an overnight thing, as you saw a little over a decade later with the success of One Direction or Little Mix on weekend talent shows.

Back then there was more of a slow drip, drip, drip of us into the public's consciousness.

Although people really don't believe it when I say we genuinely had no idea how much of an impact we were making on these children's minds and their lives.

But Party in the Park was just crazy. Even reading about it in the news the next day, we just couldn't believe it was happening. It was one of those moments where I thought, *How am I in this?*

Subsequently, it didn't seem real. For me personally anyway, going through it, when those moments happened, it all became quite dreamlike, and almost like I couldn't take it in properly.

People ask what makes a really good pop song and I think it is a good chorus with a little sprinkle of magic on top. A little bit of fluff.

My favourite song is 'Don't Stop Movin'', but the best one to actually perform would have to be 'Reach', because it is such a magical feeling to look out onto the crowd and see the fans singing the song back to you. It feels incredible.

We were shooting our first series, *Miami 7*, thirty minutes out of Miami in Fort Lauderdale, which is basically a retirement town for senior citizens – the opposite of Miami beach, where viewers were made to think we were filming. We were also staying in the apartments where we were shooting.

Every day brought new experiences and characters we'd never expected to meet.

But while being in S Club 7 was a lot of fun, it was also an incredible amount of work at times.

If we were shooting a video, we'd be on set for a minimum of eighteen hours, working from the early morning, through the day and then into the night.

One thing that was a bit of a shame was that we didn't tour much. We only really did one tour while we were in that early period of togetherness. Instead, our work was predominantly getting ready for TV shows, learning lines and making music videos. The latter would involve learning and rehearsing the dance routines so we were perfect for the day of shooting.

Obviously, we would have to learn a new dance routine for any new track that we released.

One thing I did struggle with after our first number one was the fame side of things. We had media training in the early days and would be given very small narrative script sentences to stick to. Most of the time I felt like I was doing a post-match interview, where all the players stand there and spew out the most meaningless, but meticulously thought out, un-insightful clichés known to man and then get thanked for their time. I find it all rather bizarre. In its very essence, what is the fucking point?

This version of Hannah was the one in front of the cameras all the time. But it wasn't like we had respite to then go back to being ourselves. We never got to switch off.

We went everywhere together – ALL THE TIME – and as much as I loved those people back then, that is oppressive.

It became very difficult as well in terms of time because all of our time was mapped out for us.

There was no life for us outside of S Club 7.

Someone once told me that once fame hits you, you stop progressing. It's almost like you stop developing as a person. I didn't know what it meant then, but the thought of it sends shivers up my spine now because, God that was me. I just think those years between the ages of sixteen and twenty-one are incredibly important; they're when you are on the cusp of adulthood and finding out who you really are, and when your character starts to form.

So, behind the scenes, after the euphoria dies down from your first number-one hit and pay cheque, reality hits. Some days I felt like a pretty bird living in a gilded cage.

I'm going to backtrack here to a time when I nearly got chucked out of the band, before fame or anything happened. It was really, really bad and I was unsure whether to include it here because it involves Paul, and I don't know if he ever told anybody or kept it to himself like I did previously , but it was a pivotal, almost life-wrecking moment.

During the last stage of our formation, the band was sent for another foreign trip away together to Annie Lennox and Dave Stewart's house somewhere fabulous by the Mediterranean.

They had a pool there and we were all having fun with music on, having drinks together, dancing and what have you. And then Paul and I went for a little snoop around the house.

I mean, come on, it was Annie Lennox and Dave Stewart's holiday villa, of course you're going to have a little nosey around downstairs.

So, during the course of our investigation we found our-selves in their garage, which had so many toys in it, like go-karts and a motorbike.

Well, you don't need much imagination to guess what I am about to tell you.

Stupidly, we decided to take the bike out while completely steaming, as you do when you're young and you've got no fear.

It chills me now looking back at this moment – sorry, Mum and Dad – but egging each other on, we thought it a brilliant idea to take one of these things out for a ride about.

We went riding down this mountain on the bike, and of course when you go down something you have to come back up, so we turned to get back up to the house before somebody missed us, and as we came round this one corner we were going too fast.

It was either fly off the side or go straight into the moun-tain. So Paul swerved and we went into the mountain.

There were scratches all over us, we were shaking like leaves, but incredibly we didn't have any broken bones, and most importantly, we were alive.

We thought we could get away with it and tried to cover it up. The bike was in a bad state, but still working, so we managed to get back up the mountain to the house and put the wrecked bike back in the garage.

None of the others had even noticed we'd sneaked out, and we just went to our own beds so people didn't see our scratches and bruises.

We all left the next day, us stupidly thinking we'd gotten away with it, but of course they were always going to find the bike.

And then it was just a case of coming clean.

When we confessed to our monumental idiocy, unsurprisingly it went down like a lead balloon with management.

To say they were angry was an understatement. One of the managers – whose name I can't remember for the life of me – shouted this should be the end for us.

They were livid and said we were to leave the band. They told us they were having a meeting to decide what to do. I don't know whether they already knew what they were going to do, and wanted us to stew for being such a pair of idiots, or whether they were genuinely considering kicking us out. But they let us off saying, 'You are very lucky that we've decided to keep you in. But you are really on your last ever warning.'

We were just happy to be alive to be honest. It was one of those drunk moments of just like, oh yeah, this will be fun.

The others didn't approve. I guess they wouldn't have found themselves in that situation. But that's life, isn't it?

And management would've replaced the bike and probably ordered another one and had it delivered before Dave Stewart even saw the damage.

However, to Dave and Annie, I am sorry!

Every Saturday we'd have morning shows on the likes of CD:UK with Cat Deeley and Ant and Dec.

On New Year's Day, you'd always have to film something, but I wouldn't let it stop me having fun.

I just used to roll up in whatever I was wearing. I'd never do that now.

When we were in the UK we had a little bit more freedom from each other because we were not living in a house together all the time and could go back to our own places.

But more often than not, we were away. And when we were away, we were living in the same hotel together, or in American apartments.

It was becoming increasingly difficult to have any kind of relationship with anybody outside the band – even in terms of friendship – because we were so well known.

And people thought they knew us because we were portraying these personas on the telly. It was almost like those characters had taken over our identity. So I wanted to get away from all that.

S Club 7 Hannah was the blonde, bubbly, easy-going one. So whatever that is, there's not much depth to it and there's not much character to it.

Most of the band were older than me, but Jon, Bradley and I were all around seventeen years old. Maybe because I was a late developer, I still just had so much more to work out.

On photoshoots Rachel would always get in there first and always position herself so she'd get the clothes that suited her.

But I didn't know; I just hadn't really found my style, and nobody was really helping me to get to know what it was.

I don't think that was anyone's priority. We would just be given a selection of clothes that were what they thought we should be wearing.

There would always be a whole rail. But then the stylist would have in mind roughly which outfit would go to which band member, but if you were to get in the first fitting, you might be able to change their minds and pick something yourself.

I attempted to arrive early to a shoot once, but Rachel was there already choosing the clothes she liked.

So, I didn't care. I suppose in fairness to her, she cared more about clothes and that's her thing.

You can't help but notice the little things when you are working with people so much. But it was fine at the time because it wasn't as important to me.

Tina and I hung out in the early days because obviously we got in first, so we had a connection and close bond, as we did with Paul.

I hung out with Jon quite a lot too. And we lived together in Barcelona after Paul had left.

Everyone was living in their own apartments by then, but then Jon and I decided we would prefer to share a bigger place.

Then Paul came over sometimes to see us. So we were good friends throughout those early years.

Jon and Paul, and I were a very good fit. And that was the beauty about S Club 7: you could pick who you wanted to hang out with on the day.

When it came to performing for the Queen's Golden Jubilee in 2002, I can't remember any arguments over costumes.

We were given white and silver to wear and the costumes were tailored to each of us with our own little unique look. I always liked an asymmetric top – that would be my thing – while Rachel would usually be in trousers.

She was a bit self-conscious of her legs – as lots of women are self-conscious about something when they're young. (I don't know why; her legs are great – iconic, as some FHM readers might say!) But we all have things about our bodies that niggle us.

Rachel would choose trousers over skirts, so Tina and I would often have our legs out in a skirt or dress to balance it out.

I know mine was my boobs, which I will get to later.

Anyway, there was no drama that day with the costumes. Everybody was excited to be there performing at Buckingham Palace.

My mum couldn't believe I was going to sing in front of the Queen.

It was incredible performing at the Golden Jubilee because we sang with Sir Brian May, which was just mind-blowing, and Sir Paul McCartney was there as well.

We were in the middle of London in front of a sea of people. And at the reception at the palace afterwards, a young Prince William and Harry came over to chat with us.

It did feel a little odd to start with when speaking to them. I was trying to remember what we'd been told about how to address them, but I didn't need to worry.

They were both just really amenable, and, dare I say it, normal.

William led the conversation and the three of us just went off on a small tangent about what music we liked at that point that was current.

They said they really liked listening to pop music and gave a good impression of being interested in our band and the other acts there; I think I probably spoke to them for longer than I remember. I felt that they wanted to fit into our world as much as we at that moment wanted to fit into theirs, so we all felt comfortable and on equal footing.

They didn't do that thing where they're looking over your

shoulder and eyeing up the next person. They were very present and took their time.

It felt as natural as a meeting in that grand setting could.

Mum still has an amazing photo of me standing next to Prince Harry.

When it came to the royal line up, the Queen shook all our hands and I attempted a polite curtsy.

It wasn't deep, but it was better than Liz Truss's attempt.

Everybody always asks me about meeting the Queen and what she said to us, but I'm afraid it went by in a blur.

I remember noticing she had lovely skin. I actually noticed Brian May more than the Queen.

Just his presence. I mean on stage, and I guess with the hair and everything, he just stood out in terms of making an effort.

He was friendly, as was Paul McCartney.

I loved Princess Diana, so for me it was an amazing spectacle that I will never forget, but it meant even more to me to perform with Brian May; that's what was incredible.

The palace itself was surreal, and as you'd expect, filled with amazing grand rooms, extremely high ceilings and elaborate cornices; you could look at the walls and be mesmerised by all the detailing, colour, patterns and everything like that for quite some time.

You'd just wander from massive room to massive room and everywhere was swarming with people and I hardly knew anybody.

I hoped that someone might catch my eye and start talking to me.

I did have a few too many champagnes while there, but we

were only there for about ninety minutes and then we were told that our cars were waiting outside.

If we had stayed longer we probably would have got pissed out of our heads and caused God knows what carnage, so I expect there sensibly was a time limit put on it and some nice equerries escorted us out of the exit and back to the real world.

My most exciting celebrity encounters happened, of course, in Hollywood. We had a much better time filming *LA 7* than we had in Miami.

I remember walking on the beach with Rachel and Tina. Rachel was further ahead in the distance and Robbie Williams came over and chatted with me and Tina.

I think Tina was dying inside and obviously we were very happy to be talking to him. Well, *I* was extremely happy, but when he saw Rachel, he made a beeline for her up the beach.

We watched them have a chat from a distance. There have been some rumours over the years about Robbie asking her out, more than once apparently. I don't know what the truth is, I'm afraid. Anyway, I do think he had a thing for her, and kept trying, but it never seemed to go anywhere.

With the workload we didn't really go to many parties but when we did go out, we were *out* out.

The most famous person I met was Jack Nicholson, and when I was introduced to him one night in Bel Air I thought I was so starstruck.

It was only a brief encounter, but it was the best introduction of my career.

We walked into this incredibly cool hip private party at some star's house in the hills very late one night.

It was one of those places where you have to play it with a

really cool and laid-back vibe, otherwise you'll stand out like a sore thumb.

I'd had a few drinks and was rocking a little black dress, sashaying across the room only to stop in my tracks.

In front of me was Jack, in real life, holding court with a group of people.

He looked across and gave me a look.

What a face he has. It's just Hollywood personified.

For that brief moment, time stood still.

He was chatting to somebody else and I slinked across towards him. I didn't have a clue who he was talking to or what it was about, nor did I care, but it seemed to be drying up and coming to a close.

When they said their goodbyes and walked away, Jack turned to me with that incredible expression, smiled and said 'Hi' in that distinctively Jack Nicholson way.

In my head I went, *Oh my God*, and I just wanted to stay in that spot for ever.

The voice in my brain was saying, *This is just not happening.* Another voice in my head was replying, *Just be calm, Hannah, nod, smile, but be cool.*

I mean, it's bloody Jack Nicholson!

The whole thing was wild; it was mind blowing as a kid, pretty much, that he was talking to me, and I was not taking anything he was saying in, because I just wanted to soak up the moment and enjoy the feeling of being in his presence and of being seen by him. He asked about me, and what I was up to in LA.

I was thinking, *Shit, he's just asked me something, what did he ask?* I could hardly act like I am deaf and ask him to repeat it.

That five-minute encounter seemed to last for ever, and

somehow I managed to hold it in and mention acting. To have been in a film with him would've been amazing but it was worlds away from my acting ability at the time!

Such was his power, the whole energy of the room lay with him and he didn't even have to leave his spot; people just gravitated towards him. He was the ultimate star, and I will never forget that moment.

As much as I wanted to stay standing next to him, I knew I had to play it down and walk away, so I said my goodbyes and quietly walked away to a gobsmacked Tina, Paul and Bradley, who just couldn't believe that little Hannah from S Club 7 had been hanging out with Jack Nicholson.

The band didn't leave time for much – least of all romance – but before Paul and I found each other, I enjoyed a few flings of my own.

One night at a showbiz event I met Brian McFadden from Westlife.

We'd crossed paths quite a few times and we'd always chatted backstage at events together, so we would often speak, and I guess flirt a bit, but that was it really.

I liked the way he carried himself – he had swagger. He was very tall and attractive, and a bit of a Jack the Lad, which I like, so I was pleased when he chatted me up.

He's a nice guy. We did have a couple of dates where we went out for drinks. I found him charming, naughty, entertaining and very handsome.

We may have both been in a hotel at one point together, or something like that.

But then he ghosted me. I'd thought he liked me, and wrote him a love letter to explain how I felt.

I needed to get the facts, and it turned out he was in love with Kerry Katona.

One night I went to a concert and saw him with her by his side, and he looked utterly loved up.

It was apparent from the soppy way he was staring at her that his heart was elsewhere and totally with Kerry. So it was obvious that I was a distant memory at that point!

After Brian, I went out with a different type of guy – Jack Ryder of *EastEnders* fame. We met at Elstree Studios when I was up for a *Top of the Pops* recording.

I don't remember much about his character, but he was quiet and shy, and I found him quite reserved – but after the swagger of Brian it was all very lovely. I knew we were too different for it to ever last, but I liked his face. He had a very boyish good look.

On our first date I was having my hair done at some posh hairdresser's and he came to meet me.

He was so shy and it was very short-lived. It just fizzled out; we just stopped calling each other, and he went on to marry Kym Marsh.

I found out recently that Simon Webbe from Blue had had a crush on me. We met up at an event recently and I was like, *I had no idea you liked me, Simon. Really?* He was very sweet. I wouldn't have thought I'd be his type at all, but there you go.

I never knew how to take Lee Ryan back in the day. I mean, he was definitely a ladies' man! He's a lovely guy – he lives quite close to me, and I bumped into him recently at Whole Foods in Richmond where we had a quick chat across the cash till.

There was never any rivalry with other bands like All

Saints, who were too cool for us and had their own vibe going on.

We didn't get close to many of our pop contemporaries – we never went out with Steps, for instance; it's a shame that we didn't make more of that social aspect of it, I guess.

Although I am sure if we had got to know them more, there would have been more spats!

Chapter Eight

Goodbye, Paul x

Dealing with the sadness of losing Paul has been difficult and writing this chapter is an emotional personal challenge that I have been wrestling with and putting off because it is still fresh in my mind.

The shock news of Paul's death left me shaken, upset and a bit despondent.

What is sad is that Paul seemed to just be getting on with his life, and in a good place, with lots to look forward to. It somehow makes it even more unfair that he never got to enjoy the good things that had been coming his way.

Knowing that he never tasted the happiness and unconditional love of his own little family and children – which I had hoped he'd find for himself one day – breaks my heart. He had a lot to give and was always a bit of a joker, and happy-go-lucky, which I hoped he would pass on one day. Very sadly, that wasn't meant to be.

A subject I'd like to touch on is my relationship with Paul before his death, as there has been incorrect information leaked to the press on this subject, and I'm concerned there may be more to come, so I'm going to set the record straight. It's been a hard decision to decide whether or not to discuss this but I've decided to include it for the reasons listed above, and because I feel it's a more appropriate time to discuss this as we aren't in the immediate aftermath of his passing.

The truth is, we hadn't actually spoken a word in eight years. In 2021, I received an email from Paul out of the blue, the content of which was deeply disturbing – and my only real concern was for his mental health. The trouble was that it was filled with a lot of anger and that made it very difficult to know what to do. I felt that reasoning with him was definitely not an option, and due to its content, I did not and will not share it with anybody, as it was so hurtful. Before I worked with him again, I had to seek assurances that he was okay, and that he wouldn't have a problem with us working together again.

We had a mediator facilitate our re-introduction to one another after so long, and it was extremely awkward. We left the meeting on much better terms, but the time was limited and we didn't get to sort out what was probably the underlying problems, or attempt to at least, which was a huge shame although we left the whole thing seemingly happy and with a plan.

Someone leaked this meeting to the press, and only a few days after the leak, Paul died. My initial reaction was to think that it was suicide and start blaming myself. I thought maybe he thought I was going to give his email to the press or something. I was absolutely beside myself to be honest. All these ideas going through my head and just blame, blame, blame. It was horrible. How had we gotten to this point? It was so very sad, the whole situation. If you ever have the power to take a situation by the horns and fix it, do it – you might never get the chance again.

Paul was Mr S Club 7. He embodied the friendly, exciting and positive ethos of the band and we could not have achieved the mammoth success we did without him.

And sorry to upset anybody, but I feel the band was lesser without Paul. It wasn't the same after he left and it will never be the same again.

He was the heart of that band in more ways than he'll ever know.

But more than that, he was an absolute monumental part of my time here on this planet and of my development and growth as a person.

Only Paul understood that time we were together in the way that I can because we went through those things together.

What we had was five quite intense years at the most formative stage of our lives.

All of our experiences that we share, in bad times and good, shape us in some way or form – whether we want them to or not – and being with Paul certainly impacted my life.

We were just a pair of lucky theatre kids who were thrown together in some bizarre twist of fate in the weird world of show business, and we made the best of it, I guess.

This is my tribute to him.

He was my first serious relationship, and up to that moment the first man I'd told I loved, apart from my darling dad, and meant it.

We grew up together. It was a very special time in our lives and no one can take that love we shared away from us.

I didn't set out to bag myself an S Club 7 boyfriend. There was never a romantic movie-style moment whereby I woke up and thought I was in love with Paul and ran into the street to tell him.

The awareness that I had developed feelings for him crept up on me slowly.

It wasn't until we had spent time together in America that I started to really notice that I had feelings for Paul that may have gone beyond that of a deep friendship.

Things started to slowly develop between us as friends in a slow manner that we enjoyed and savoured, having the power of youth and years ahead, rather than behind us.

There had been a little frisson during that misjudged motorbike crash abroad two years earlier, but I brushed it aside as being from the adrenaline rush and drama of escaping being killed that night. There was never an 'oh look at him, he's fit, I need to be with that man at all costs' level of attraction towards him.

So no, I did not fancy Paul in the initial days of S Club 7.

You may not believe me, but I was so young when we started the band – I just wasn't thinking about dating.

What's more, I looked like a twelve-year-old boy, and so to me Paul was just my *Pendragon* pal. But it's strange how things change.

When we were filming *LA 7*, Paul would hire a car and we'd go on these long drives in California. We used to drive up into the hills and chill together, and talk about the astrologer Jonathan Cainer. Paul had a book by Cainer and it sounds really *woo woo*, so you can laugh, but we would read up on our star signs and forecasts. He loved doing that, and in later years really got into it.

There were a lot of these gorgeous little hippie stores in LA where we would spend the rare spare hours that we had away from work.

There were also a lot of vinyl stores at the West Hollywood flea markets. So on a Sunday morning we would enjoy going to those together and sifting through all the records.

Music was where we really connected and we shared the same taste. We were into sort of similar vibes – bands like the Red Hot Chili Peppers and Fleetwood Mac.

It was a golden time that felt like my coming of age. I was still only eighteen, growing and developing and learning about myself, and Paul was five years older.

I always looked up to him, and obviously at that point he would never have seen me in a romantic way because before I turned nineteen I was just a kid.

So it took a long time for him to fall for me. It took spending time – a lot of time – together to develop those feelings.

And practically, it wasn't like either of us could have had a normal relationship outside of the band. We couldn't really date anybody else anyway, as our workload was all-consuming, so we were lucky to develop this connection.

But during that intense time we spent in America, we kept a lot of it hidden from our bandmates. And it was just insane, because after our bonding sessions in LA, it was obvious to anyone that saw us together that we were more than just good friends.

My good friend Neil, who Sheridan and I had been living with when I was back in London, was also Paul's best friend. He reminded me as I was writing this book how Paul thought he had got away with hiding it from him, completely unaware that Neil and Sheridan had already guessed.

Paul and I shared our first kiss by accident, during a drunken moment.

A big group of us went skiing together which included Jon from the band, Neil, Paul, Sheridan, my sister, her boyfriend and some friends of hers.

One of my sister's friends and Paul took a bit of a shine to each other on the slopes, and to my surprise I realised that I felt territorial over him.

So after hitting the cocktails during the après-ski, I found myself dancing with Paul on the club dance floor and we had one of those classic drunk moments and fell into each other for a quick snog.

But then we were both mortified we had allowed the drunken snog to happen.

We probably didn't want to upset the dynamics of the band, I imagine, so that's why it had taken so long for it to happen.

After our holiday and before I headed back to America, Neil and I had a conversation and I opened up to him fully, because I was starting to get these feelings of jealousy when Paul was getting with these other people, and I didn't know what to do.

I turned to him to help me as Paul's friend, because Paul and I were not an item and so I had no right to be jealous of who he hooked up with.

Neil took one look at my soppy face and said, 'Honey, you've just got to tell him. You just gotta tell Paul about how you feel.'

He was right, but that's easier said than done.

When we got back to America, I kept trying to find the

right moment to pluck up the courage to tell him about my feelings.

I was so nervous he was going to reject me and I'd lose an amazing friend – not to mention the nightmare it would cause in the band.

I seized my moment when we went out for one of our special drives. We parked up to admire the view and I finally told him.

It wasn't a direct proposition, more a convoluted story about how he and I had known each other for so long.

Paul still didn't seem to have any suspicions as I said I had something to ask him, and I babbled away, saying something like, 'Hey, what I am about to say to you is embarrassing'.

'Hannah, you know you can tell me anything, so what's the matter?'

By that point I couldn't turn back. As embarrassing as it felt, these feelings I was having for him were not going to leave me.

So I explained that I had to do something about it and find out if he was in the same place as me, because otherwise I might just have to make a sharp exit out of the band and flee the country in disgrace.

As soon as I got the words out, I had this overwhelming urge to kiss him and wanting him to be mine.

To my utmost relief, he looked delighted and confessed that he had been battling his feelings for me. We decided to explore things – just the two of us.

We both started laughing at our self-inflicted anguish of the heart and then enjoyed a good snog.

When we managed to prise ourselves apart to come up

for air, we discussed our worries about the rest of the band finding out about us. I don't think any of the other girls liked him, so I didn't think it would be a problem. Management's take on it however, might be quite different, we suspected!

And when we were performing as a band on stage, some girls would go crazy and throw things in a bid to get him to take notice of them, which was definitely something that took some getting used to!

Anyway, we spent the next six months sneaking around, ridiculously, even though I think Neil had posted about it in our friendship group's instant messaging forum (WhatsApp hadn't been invented yet!) and it became the worst kept secret in the world.

Once we were open with each other, friends would say things like, 'Oh, I remember when you rang me. You told me this about so and so like a girlfriend would do.'

And I said, 'Did I?' I can't remember saying anything because I'd just blocked my feelings out as much as I could.

So our friends knew we liked each other before we did!

I mean, the kisses were *just sort of* happening by then. We'd had enough drunken kisses too; we were playing out boyfriend and girlfriend but we weren't official.

It naturally progressed to a point where if either of us were to go with someone else, it would feel wrong.

Looking back on it all now – more than twenty years later – it feels such a sweet and innocent time.

We were young and carefree together. We used to say I love you all the time to each other.

His pet name for me was 'Monkey'. He used to call me his cheeky monkey and say 'I love you, Monkey.' I'd call him

'Sport'. Nothing super cute. Although I also used to call him 'Poo', which we used to find quite endearing, weirdly. Our funny little names rolled off the tongue easily. It was very, very innocent.

It was very natural and we felt like soulmates who had found each other and intertwined. Our energies had aligned and we said we were each other's twin flame. We'd talk about everything and nothing, the way lovers do, and he was, I suppose, my trusted person in the band who had my back, someone I could turn to when the shit hit the fan. When I was having a down day or something, I knew he'd catch me and make the world a bit of a brighter place.

He loved driving me everywhere and I felt safe and cared for in his presence.

So the first time Paul and I got together was in America. It all felt very special because we were so in love.

Everything just clicked for us in every area and our love kept growing.

After we got together we were of course still working together in the band, so I made the sensible decision, I think, that we should keep our own apartments. It was good to have our separate spaces so that we weren't always on top of each other (literally and figuratively . . .) – but of course we had the freedom to go over to each other's homes as and when we wanted.

We did not spend every night together. I sometimes wanted time to myself and he would have wanted some space too. We were very easy going with each other and our needs.

If we needed to let off steam, we'd give each other room to do that, and some nights we'd fall asleep curled up on the sofa and wake up wrapped in one another's arms at 2 a.m.

Paul was not going to let me go back to my respective house at that time, so more often than not I'd end up staying there and he'd carry me to bed.

When we were abroad on holiday, we loved going off exploring together and it was lovely to fall asleep together every night.

When it came to telling the others in the band about us, it went smoothly – thank goodness.

We were nervous, but we sat them all down and Paul took the lead and said, 'I think you guys already know that Hannah and I have been spending a lot of time with each other lately, and we've decided to officially make a go of it and wanted to tell you we're together.'

No one was the least surprised by this announcement, and thankfully there were no meltdowns, tears or any issues at all. Well, they knew already, really – like all our other friends – as our chemistry together was so obvious.

Everyone just dealt with it and got on with it.

I mean what could they have done to stop us? Nothing. Two people like each other and that's it, so it was fine.

And of course, they were happy for us.

It was just such a relief for it to be out in the open. But then we had to tell management – and we weren't sure if they would approve.

I'm sure management were thinking, *shit, how are we going to handle this?* Then the execs had a brain wave. They decided that they would start to write it into the plot of the TV show, so life imitated art – or in this case, art imitated life.

Anyway, that is how the character of Hannah came to go out with the character of Paul. And it worked, because the ratings went through the roof.

Up to that point, we had not had it too bad in the tabloids, considering what we had got up to.

One time they wanted to write I was a lesbian.

Paul and I wanted to keep it quiet and private from the press, but somebody had found out, and to try and get the story that we were a couple, a paper told our management that they were planning to say I was a lesbian the next day unless I came clean. They didn't run the story, which was clearly rooted in an outdatedand, frankly ridiculous homophobic trope that all lesbians had short hair – I had short hair at the time and they thought they could get away with it.

They never did write that in the end.

Or it would be silly made-up stories about our supposedly racy sex lives.

We just ignored it all.

From fans, I don't remember getting any negative feedback either, although some must have noticed how close we were. It was always positive, although we did worry that our bubble would be burst by a tabloid headline without a moment's notice.

During our relationship when we were both in the band, it was for the most part very happy.

We saw the world together, hung out and cooked together as much as we were able to. It was a rosy time because we were carefree and young with zero responsibilities.

I loved that he would pick up his guitar in the apartment and sit strumming it while I danced around the room, or we would lie for hours listening to music, talking about our dreams for after the band.

I wanted to get back to acting, he wanted to continue to make music.

So why did he decide to leave S Club 7?

A simple reason: he was deeply unhappy. He was never comfortable with his position in the band. I think there was resistance from the start. Ultimately, Paul never dreamed of being in a pop band; he had dreams of a different sort of music, so S Club 7 never felt right for him.

Over time, his frustration built up to a point where he had to leave – he just couldn't face one more day of it.

The fame was another difficult aspect to deal with. It just wasn't good for his soul. We'd be chased by paparazzi – they tried to get into hotel rooms, and we would be paranoid that our car was being followed or bugged because they would always be there waiting for us, wherever we went.

Singing in S Club 7 for the rest of his life wasn't what he wanted to do.

Don't misconstrue this as him being embarrassed about being in the band. Absolutely not. He loved all of us and the times we had together, but he had grown up and he was heavily into his alternative music, I guess you'd call it. He had such strong opinions on what he liked in art and our music didn't align with or represent him as an individual.

It was difficult watching him struggle with his decision over whether to leave or stay.

When we started the band, we never knew when we would call it a day. We had signed a five-year contract, and to break it early would mean a huge loss of earnings.But for Paul, who had known this wasn't his passion from the beginning, it reached a point where everything became too much.

Obviously I knew it was coming, but I think we all knew in our hearts that Paul would want to leave first, because his heart was never one hundred per cent in the band.

He was very open about his dreams and desires, so it felt obvious and natural to me that one day he would finally pluck up the courage and go.

Sometimes Paul and I would go back to one of our apartments after a studio recording or a public appearance and have some downtime after the day's events, listen to some music, mess about, watch a movie, whatever. It was normal – just like any couple who get back after a busy day at work and have a little moan and enjoy their downtime.

It's to be expected from being in just about any job.

So Paul and I would take it in turns choosing a takeout, and then we might get whatever had been bugging us that day off our chests. It would be the tiniest things, those minor irritations can build up and explode if they are not dealt with.

It just became part of our daily conversation.

But then it started to become bigger than the day-to-day complaints, and you could see it in his physicality: something was not right, and it was eating him away inside.

He started chatting about his problems with the direction of the band more, taking issue with pointless things that had niggled him, that wouldn't have bothered him when he was his normal happy self. He'd react to things negatively, and I realised that he was becoming miserable about the stuff we were doing at work. I would use my intuition to identify which of his small grievances were really significant, and I encouraged him to do something about them – rather than just complaining and growing ever more unhappy.

He especially struggled – as is to be expected – with having to show a different facade to the public. We had a contractual obligation to be our characters when out in public, and to be mindful of the band and the responsibility that carries – especially towards our young fans.

I think it just got a bit exhausting for him, not to be free flowing. It was quite a difficult thing to watch, because from my perspective, it felt like he was being inauthentic and having to fake believing in something he wasn't into anymore.

The energy at home was not ruined by his moods – nothing like that. I know people say being around people when they are down can bring you down, but Paul didn't inflict that on others. He put everything on himself, and put on a brave face for everybody else.

And he didn't ever call in sick or do a Robbie Williams when he left Take That and went off the rails, or a Zayn Malik when he left One Direction and embarked on a solo pop career straight after leaving.

Everyone just knew he wasn't feeling it anymore.

It might sound quite bizarre, because obviously we were in a very privileged situation to be in a massive hit band, getting number-one records and having thousands of adoring fans following our every move. Kids go on talent shows today in the hope of making it and getting just a taste of the lifestyle we had, and to some on the outside it might have looked like Paul was ungrateful for all our success, fame and wealth. I can understand that they would have questioned his decision.

He was probably quite excited to see us every day, and while I know he loved all of us most of the time – even when he and Bradley would have their spats, only to make up minutes later like best friends do when they've been too long in each other's company – he was growing tired and bored.

But Paul did appreciate everything being in the band had given him (apart from the fame he wasn't keen on) he knew that was never going to go away. He was bored and wanted to make different music.

The thing that stopped him from walking out the door every day was the financial aspect.

One evening after dinner, I asked what his plan was regarding money.

I advised him that he had to be realistic about how long his earnings would last in the real world and how he would support himself once they ran out.

He thought about it and then he landed a deal before he quit with a band called Skua. It wasn't like a massive record deal, and he wasn't really promised anything big, but it gave him faith that things would be OK.

And that's what Paul lived off I think – faith. He was a dreamer. He didn't drag his heels when it came to his passions. And he was a very deep thinker.

I would try to advise him and say, 'Try to keep going a little longer, to when they all want to call it a day and then you'll be much better off?'

I encouraged him to think about the financial security seeing the band through to the end would bring.

'But, as your girlfriend,' I said, 'I completely understand if you really can't wait another year to call it a day?'

And like I said, he didn't know how long we were going to carry on for – none of us did. He'd say, 'I can't handle it any longer, Hannah, it's only going to get more difficult.'

I wish I had pushed harder to persuade him to stay. I just wanted to tell him what would make him happy again.

I guess he thought he had it all figured out, but maybe he hadn't thought it through properly. Quitting when he did ruined him to some extent – it didn't give him the freedom he'd hoped for largely because of the financial sacrifice of early severance.

People have asked if I wanted to marry Paul back then, but the answer is no. I didn't ever have dreams of getting married as a little girl, and I was still working myself out. I hadn't really considered having children yet either. I knew I wanted kids, but not yet. I was very, very young. I was finding my feet, figuring out who I was and learning one thing and another with Paul.

I mean, I was barely looking after myself, and with being in the band and feeling like my own growth had been sort of put on hold, I needed to come back to life.

But Paul and I worked well together when we were in the band because there were certain parts of our personalities that really did get on. It was like being a student at university: we were carefree with no responsibilities. Somebody told you where to go at what time, and took care of shit. We didn't have any big decisions to make together and I think that's why in the real world we struggled a bit; once he'd left the band, we didn't survive quite as well.

We'd gotten together in an environment where everything was done for us, where we didn't have anything to worry about in terms of stress or paying bills. When we weren't working, we could sit enjoying listening to music for three hours without a care in the world.

But in a scenario where, you know, you have to do shit and sort stuff out, are those two people going to be able to be as free?

And Paul was like a big kid. He needed more of a maternal-type partner. I loved the way he sung and could just pick up a guitar, but real life requires more than sitting playing the guitar all day. Perhaps being in a band so young convinced us otherwise.

In adult life, there's a lot less time for that. You may even have kids that need taking care of; food needs to go on the table.

Unfortunately, the practical side of life takes over and I wanted someone more hands-on.

Paul took a long time finding his direction and sadly, outside the band, things didn't bode so well for us.

When I got my acting career back up and running and I was back in America making my own Hollywood film away from Paul, I enjoyed the freedom and knew I was starting to toy with the idea of single life.

People weren't seeing our home life, and it was a mess. I was a slobbish person back then too, so in some aspects we were well suited to each other. But I came to realise that it only worked when we were living in hotels with someone to do everything for us.

I think that's how our relationship survived five years at the age we both were.

If S Club 7 hadn't happened and I was single now, would I have fancied him if I had seen him on the street? If he was a gigging musician and had his own shit together, and if I had had my own shit together, then probably, yes.

The second time we got back together took me completely by surprise. I find this hard to write about, because I regret the pain and hurt it caused to my now-partner, Adam at the time.

I was going through my own challenges with health when S Club 7 reformed in 2015 and seeing Paul took me back to that point in time before all the bad stuff had happened.

And I went back to Paul. It was comfort, escapism maybe.

We tried to stop. We tried to stop it but the force between us at that point was bigger than life. He was like a storm that would blow into my life causing carnage.

But once the tour was over and we went back to trying to date in the real world again, without directions and a timetable to stick to, I quickly realised he wasn't in as great a place in his life as I had thought, and had not changed at all. But then I wasn't in that great a place either.

I couldn't put up with the lack of oomph, general procrastination and lack of direction.

Then some hurtful things were said when we broke up, and eventually Adam and I got back together.

I'd say he was a troubled soul at times. He clearly wasn't in a great place when he went to the papers about me and said some deeply hurtful things. Things obviously felt so misaligned for him that he needed to change things up, I guess.

Paul wasn't depressed, but he did have some demons to battle. He could find it difficult to talk about something very personal.

Being in the band at a young age meant that management had so much power over us, our lives were in their hands, and outside of that, Paul just couldn't adapt to life back in the real world.

I felt as much as he wanted to have it, he had no autonomy over his life, even when he was free of the band.

And that's the tragedy of it. From being the first to want to escape that control, he was the one keenest and seemingly happy to go back to it, and I wonder if that was some sub-conscious desire to be free of personal responsibility and have someone take care of him again.

But when we met up early in 2023 to apologise to each other and make amends for our hurtful behaviour, he seemed in a better place.

We shared a massive hug and he asked about my children and wanted to see their photos.

It felt good to put the past behind us and have closure on that chapter; to shut the door on what had been almost ten years of our lives together.

He was DJing and having fun with his friends and looking for love and a family of his own, I guess.

He was my best friend. All I ever wanted was for him to find true love and happiness.

I hope, Paul, wherever you are now, you are at peace. Thank you for being you and for everything.

Chapter Nine

Breaking Up Is Hard to Do

A fter Paul quit the band, I was in a bit of a quandary. I still had him at home, but I was upset that I'd lost my best pal at work and it would be strange being on the road working without him to turn to and give me a hug or make a funny face to make me laugh when the others weren't looking.

We'd committed as a group to keep going sans Paul because we wanted to make the film *Seeing Double* with Gareth Gates.

The film was total tosh but Jon and I had a blast living it up together in Barcelona, where we shot it.

Management also wanted new music from us, and we had to heavily promote the film.

But I started to feel tired in the way that Paul had a year previously, and at the back of my mind I was wondering how to successfully transition from pop singer to actress; making the film confirmed that acting, not singing pop music in a recording studio, was where my heart lay.

I spoke to Paul about whether it was the right time for me to go. He could see I was losing my enthusiasm for the band, just as he once had, and that I was starting to go through the motions. I felt jaded and washed up at the tender age of twenty-three. Before then I'd always been the most excitable one in the group, ready to spring into action for whatever we needed to do as a band. I'd never complained or had to be dragged kicking or screaming into a situation; I just got on with it.

Now my tiredness was affecting me and I felt despondent being in the band, like Paul had done. Spending nearly five years away from family and missing birthdays, births, engagements and weddings is hard.

I was becoming irritable with Paul too, and showing the strain from when the alarm would go off at 4 a.m. and I'd be on a plane to Aberdeen for a radio show before flying back to London to attend a premiere.

'Hannah, I think you've outgrown it,' he said one evening, pouring me a large glass of wine as I kicked my heels off and slumped on the sofa.

He'd wanted to go to a gig that night to watch some alternative bands, but it was the last thing I wanted to do. Plus, I was on *GMTV* with Lorraine Kelly the following morning and needed to put on my cheery early morning 'I'm happy to be here' face, or management would smell a rat.

How to fix it? I wasn't brave or – in my head – reckless enough to do what Paul had done and just say fuck this and walk off. As I said, I still disagreed with Paul's decision to walk out from a financial perspective. It cost him heavily to not have stayed the course with us to the end, but he did what was right in his heart, so I respected that, and he seemed happier recording with Skua than he had with us – despite their lack of commercial success.

We chatted and he suggested finding an acting agent and for me to start having a scout around to line something up.

'Hannah, all the others will be looking to go soon and will be putting feelers out after the film, so what's the harm in you doing it?'

From that day on, behind the scenes I was plotting how to do just that and get back into the drama world. I linked up with an acting agent who was scouting for me and lining up auditions.

And Paul was right – the others were getting itchy feet too.

It became apparent that other people in the band were keen to try their hands at different things and we were all yearning to go our separate ways.

Part of me wanted to wrap it up, but financially it was better for me to stay those extra few months.

Our band had sold ten million records worldwide by that point and it seemed madness to pull the plug on that before the five years were up.

My dad called me and said, 'Hannah, you'll be silly to leave now, because it's going to finish in a year's time anyway. Just get through this last bit and then do what you really want to do with your life.'

I am glad I listened.

I casually asked the others if they were interested in continuing beyond 2003 to gauge their appetites. Everybody wanted out, and Rachel appeared to have already been putting a career as a solo artist into motion. We unilaterally agreed, having sold millions of records, had several number ones, won Brit awards and made a film, that we wanted to go out on a high after five years, so we sat down and all agreed we'd hang up our microphones for good in October 2003 and announce it at a concert. We knew the tabloids would soon pick the story up, spreading the news wider to fans across the country.

Management took it well, I thought, although it was hard to tell from Simon's face.

People assume when you're in a band selling millions of records you must be coining it in, but they don't realise that when you sign these multi-million-pound contracts, the money management shells out on your wardrobe, styling, make-up, hair, limos, first-class flights, five-star hotels, entertaining, and the rest, all comes out of your deal.

Your money is being splashed on what is a lovely lifestyle but really is wastage.

For at the end of that three-, four-, or five-year deal they deduct all that expenditure from the total, and what is left is your earnings. And then the tax man comes along to take a further chunk of it! It really isn't the path to wealth and riches people imagine it is.

Nevertheless, I was glad to get out relatively unscathed.

Following our split, my new acting agent put me up for a part in a film, *Agent Cody Banks 2: Destination London*, playing a spy.

The best part about it was that filming took place just outside London, at Knebworth House in Hertfordshire, where I could come home at night instead of being stuck in LA without Paul. It was also great to work with Anthony Anderson, who played Derek Bowman; he really kept everyone geared up on set and ready for action.

The most memorable moment of the shoot was when Keith Allen – Lily Allen's dad – apparently didn't turn up to film. A driver told me he'd gone to pick Keith up earlier that morning and found him lying in the road outside his house with his head on the curb, completely out of it, holding a nearly empty bottle of whisky. I liked this guy already!

I thought immediately of what management's reaction would be like if one of us did that and keeled over in the back of the car laughing. In fact there was one time they were showing us our newly finished music video at the Four Seasons in LA and I had gotten so shitfaced prior to the viewing that I had to sprint into a bathroom half way through the showing and projectile vomited everywhere. Oh yeah, classy me!

Disappointingly for me, I didn't have any big scenes with Keith, just a few group scenes, and we never spoke. I think he is an absolute legend, not to mention a brilliant actor, and he's hilarious.

His son Alfie – who went on to play Theon Greyjoy in *Game of Thrones* – was also in the film, though he hadn't done much acting at that point but soon made up for it and I've seen him now and again over the years to say hello.

Although the film was a little forgettable, I felt right at home on the set and had no desire to go back to S Club.

I didn't realise quite how exhausting being in the group had been until I left and went back to acting. It felt so good that I could finally be me and have freedom over my life again which was bliss.

After that I was cast in the horror flick *Seed of Chucky* with Jennifer Tilly. I loved acting in it as I had, bizarrely, been a massive fan of the *Child's Play* franchise when I was little.

With Chucky they still used puppetry and that was lovely

to see because it's now more common to have CGI in that sort of film. My scenes were easy to do, and I had a bit of time off so I could explore the country – it was the first time I'd been in LA without the band. I loved it.

Chapter Ten

Connor and Abby

Working on *Agent Cody Banks 2* and *Seed of Chucky* confirmed to me that acting was where my future was, and I couldn't wait to land another role.

The universe seemed to answer my prayers because pretty quickly an audition came up for a new ITV sci-fi series called *Primeval*.

I remember being out in a cafe some time in 2005 when my then-acting agent called me to say they wanted me to audition for this new science fiction show ITV were doing, and that it had dinosaurs in it.

'We think it's called *Primeval*, or something like that – the name keeps changing – and we're putting you forward for the lead female role of Abby.'

I'd torn off a piece of scrap paper in the cafe and scribbled down the words 'Prime Me' instead of *Primeval*, and the name Abby.

After the audition, I popped it into a treasure box I keep for sentimental things – I'm a bit of a hoarder – and there it has stayed hidden ever since.

The audition itself was one of those ones when you just don't expect anything to happen, so you make zero to little effort. I dressed in low-key attire, wearing a pair of old baggy jeans. For some reason I was into thin layering at the time—very Trinny and Susannah – so I wore a long T-shirt with a thin blue jumper over the top. My hair had been cut into a cute pixie cut and coloured bright blonde – very much as it had been in my young S Club 7 days.

So, with my new hair and casual outfit, I went along to read for the director, Cilla Ware.

Then we read again, which is a good sign. Sometimes when actors go into auditions and directors just mutter, 'OK, thanks', you know instantly that you haven't gotten it.

This time Cilla directed me more and asked if I could do it 'a little bit this way' or try 'a little bit that way'.

I got home to Paul in Brighton that evening and said, 'I'm not sure how it went, it's too hard to tell.'

The next day, to my great delight, I got a call back to come and audition with the show dinosaur, Rex.

CGI was a big part of the show and Abby had to do a lot of close-up work with a little *Tyrannosaurus rex*. This required me to do some play acting and improvisation against a green screen.

Whatever I did must have worked because I was then asked to attend a third audition. My agent prepared me for more scenes and revealed that I was to read with another actor, Andrew-Lee Potts, to test our chemistry, because most of my scenes would be with his character, Connor.

Andrew-Lee Potts? I thought. The name rings a bell. Didn't Sheridan know a guy called Andrew-Lee Potts?

I'd just have to wait and see, and went about putting heart and soul into learning my lines, until I walked into the audition room.

'Oh 'ello, Andrew,' I thought as he stood up and smiled at me.

'Hannah, I can't believe it, how long has it been?'

My eyes immediately recognised him as Sheridan's mate, who I shared an awkward kiss with a decade ago. Now all grown up, he hadn't blossomed too badly, and Cilla must have picked up on a chemistry of sorts between us at the time.

The whole thing felt a little bizarre. Reading lines with a guy I barely knew but has also kissed many moons ago all while trying to show them I was born to play Abby.

Thankfully, Cilla only made us read the scene once – no idea how to read into that – but to my delight, that night I got the call to say I was in the show.

I jumped for joy and Paul opened the champagne to celebrate. He was so excited and happy for me.

Our script said Connor loved Abby. But Abby was a bit too cool for Connor, so I thought, *Phew, no kissing scenes, it'll be fine. We'll just be friends, on and off the show.* Then again, I didn't even know if he'd been cast alongside me.

With that comforting thought, I plunged straight into becoming Abby, giving her everything I had.

And for the first few months, Andrew and I were just work mates. The crew and cast on the show quickly became a family, which is a wonderful atmosphere when working on a production. We began to go out as a gang after filming, and in that time Andrew and I slowly got to know each other. We'd all go out clubbing in London, or as a group to the pub.

Initially I thought he fancied our co-star Lucy Brown, who played Claudia, because he used to flirt with Lucy all the time and they would hang out in each other's trailers. It became increasingly difficult to go out and enjoy myself with the cast and crew because mine and Paul's relationship was rapidly deteriorating at home.

At the beginning of working on *Primeval* I had a lot of conversations with my co-star James Murray, as my relationship with Paul was weighing heavily on me. We'd have heart-to-hearts and I told James, 'Look, I'm in this relationship and I'm not happy, it's been five years and I just don't know what to do.'

James listened and kindly pointed out that I *did* know what I needed to do, which was to take responsibility for my feelings and tell Paul I had been having doubts about us.

Feeling sick with dread, I forced myself back down to Brighton to see him at the weekend and sat him down for a serious talk.

He didn't seem surprised when I said, 'Look, I'm not happy and as much as it might not be right for me, I really also don't think it's right for you either. We're just not being the best version of ourselves with each other. Do you know what I mean?'

It was hard – he said he was devastated – but he agreed and said he knew it was the right call for both of us, and if I hadn't pulled the plug he probably never would have done anything about it.

We both cried and hugged again, but in our hearts we knew our relationship had burned itself out. I told him I'd move out, and I did around two weeks later.

Coming back to set the next week, it felt like a weight had been lifted and I could focus on enjoying my work again. The opposite sex was the last thing on my mind at this point and so things moved very slowly between myself and Andrew after that but we did grow closer as the months went by, until one day he asked me out on our first date. Shortly after that, he presented me with a sweet necklace and asked me to be his girlfriend.

So being a real-life couple just worked, even though the characters we were playing didn't accurately reflect exactly what was happening in real life. In fact, in the first series, my character Abby is just like, 'Oh my God, stay the fuck away from me, Connor.' In hindsight, maybe Abby was right, but then again, it wouldn't have taken much to improve on some of my life's decisions early on! No slight on Andrew or anyone else for that matter, but perhaps just an acknowledgement of my life experience, or lack of it, shall we say.

We never tried to make things complicated for our colleagues, and never wanted anybody to feel awkward when working, so we'd play down our relationship around the others, acting still like mates instead of a couple in the honeymoon stages.

Andrew and I never brought our romance onto the set – even though we shared a Winnebago with a bed in it, we were always so professional when working.

We all shared our troubles and all the cast members were good friends. And, for a long time, there was good energy; we all just got on as a group really well. The absence of any sex scenes and the fact that Primeval was an innocent show in that respect made things a lot easier to avoid any awkwardness.

Kissing your co-star – depending on who it is – can be awkward. If you feel comfortable and if you've known them for a reasonable length of time, obviously that helps.

Truth be told, in my career I haven't really had to do that many. I also think when you have to do something and you're committed to it (and there's a whole crew watching you anyway), you just don't think about it. Even if it feels awkward, you just accept it, and think, *What else can you do to make it better? Let's just get it done.*

I think the worst would be kissing scenes with someone you're not that keen on in a play or musical in the theatre when you have to repeat it every night. Absolute nightmare! Although I guess if you get lucky, depending on the other person, it could be the best part of the job.

But most actors, I think, would say it's one of the harder parts of the job. Because even if you like your co-star, you've still got all the crew watching, and that's uncomfortable. In fairness, they do try to make it as skeletal a crew as possible for intimate scenes, but it's still not a sexy thing to have a guy with a camera watching you pretend to get it on with somebody else. I suppose it could be, if that's what you're into. But to me, it's just not that pleasant.

Nevertheless, working on *Primeval* felt utterly magical. Being on that show, it felt like things were aligning very nicely for me, and that was really good. I'd always wanted to act, and here I was playing a role that was way beyond what I'd ever anticipated doing in terms of cool characters. I think we were all so ridiculous and a bit eccentric in our own sorts of little ways, that's why the show worked.

Our cast was full of actors of a far higher calibre than me, which was great because I was able to learn so much from them and the directors. I was in an environment where I could just watch and progress every day. And that to me was an absolute privilege as every day I learned something different and really began to hone my ability as an actor.

It just felt like I was finally on a path I'd chosen because I was doing something that I had always wanted to do – playing a character that I really believed in, surrounded by an outstanding team of talented people.

I was the baby on that show. I was the one who could say, 'Oh, I like the way you do that', or 'Oh, I'll try that', and soak up the other actors' techniques like a sponge.

S Club was great in other ways, and I was very lucky to be in it, but by the end I was eager to learn and grow as an actress.

Initially, I hadn't wanted to go straight into acting after S Club, because I had a few nerves around that time. I felt like I needed to take acting lessons before launching into a new career on stage or screen. And as I wanted to get away from media and fame and all that sort of thing, a lot was up in the air.

The phone was ringing non-stop for me when I came out of S Club and I didn't answer it. I turned down so many opportunities. I don't know how many; the phone would go and I'd just ignore it.

It sounds terrible, but I really didn't feel ready. But I should have just got on the phone to my agent and said that, instead of burying my head in the sand.

But with *Primeval*, I was ready for it and ready to embrace the opportunity I was very lucky to have been afforded.

I had the confidence in *Primeval* to realise that yes, another person could have played my role, possibly better than me, but they'd have done it in a different way. I had confidence in what I was bringing to the table. And it wasn't just 'Hannah from S Club', because I knew that Cilla had liked my vibe as well.

My confidence grew from a mix of stuff. Reflecting on it now, I was so green when I was in *Agent Cody Banks 2*. I rushed into it too soon after S Club and would have taken a different approach if I had my time again. I look back at that film with some embarrassment. I remember another actor, James Faulkner, in the film coming up to me on set and asking, 'Have you thought about what you are going to do with the character?' And honestly, although I knew then that it was totally normal for actors to ask other actors that, I just hadn't a clue. So, I did need to go back to the drawing board and just work on everything.

I went to the Actor's Centre and did loads of workshops and got together with actor friends to get that little bit of inner confidence to know that I wasn't just being cast because I'd come out of a bestselling pop group and would potentially garner extra publicity.

What was also nice about *Primeval* is that the fame wasn't as extreme as it was in S Club. Comic Cons presented a great platform to socialise in a healthy, respectful manner with fans from the sci-fi world. It was a far cry from the often frantic nature of concerts. They would want to have a conversation, and they'd have questions about the character and the show.

It was just a bit of a different type of fan I guess. But I could handle that a bit better. I think if social media had been around during our time in S Club I would've struggled with it. As social media is a prerequisite for work and business nowadays, it almost can't be avoided. But if it wasn't so integral, let's just say it's something I'm still adjusting to and I could drop in a heartbeat. In all honesty, I cringe at just about every post I put out. I just find it so self-indulgent as a concept. She says as she's knowingly embarking on about a million posts! :-s

When the press learned I was dating Andrew, they would follow us in our cab when we left a bar or club. The appetite's not not as vicious these days because people are so prolific on their Instagram and TikTok, which is good – celebrities today have a bit more agency and control over their image and personal lives.

So here I was, doing my dream job.

My character was still very much there to the end, but it was never quite the same on the show after Dougie left. He was an absolute class act. He did series one, two and three. We had some good episodes in the two series after that, and great people, but I was ready to take a break.

I don't want to say I was happy that it ended, but my own personal circumstances, combined with things like Dougie leaving, may have left me feeling a little like that. Disillusioned, one might say. Obviously it's lovely to bring in new energy and different perspectives, but there's so much fondness for the first group of people involved in a show because you never know how it's going to go; there is this strong connection among the original team because we created something quite special together.

In the show we were running around in the forests in Ireland, where we filmed it, and doing all this stupid crazy stuff, and Andrew would have to say all these long words, often having no idea what he was talking about. Yet it ends up working out, and you're like, *oh my God*. And when it is completely new – as that show was – you go in with no expectations, and the beauty of it is seeing how well it all turns out.

But sadly, all good things have a habit of coming to an end.

It would've been lovely to do more because it was a very, very, very good time of my life, but it ended at the right time as my relationship with Andrew was becoming . . . let's just say we were no longer in our honeymoon period.

If we were to do more Primeval and if me and Andrew wanted to stay together, it was going to become difficult.

So I almost felt like that was my reason for going: even though I loved and I never wanted it to end from a relationship point of view, working together every day and living together was becoming difficult.

We decided to take a holiday to Portugal just to get away for a bit, and rekindle the flames, when I received the shock of my life.

Andrew proposed!

He had planned it all, unbeknown to me, taking me out on this boat, just the two of us and the boat crew.

We were floating in the sea when he dropped down on one knee and started to make a romantic speech about how he wanted to spend the rest of his life with me.

I won't bore you with it all, as I'm sure you get the gist.

However, this drunken party boat came sailing past, blasting music and whooping and cheering, as Andrew was being drowned out whilst attempting to get his words of love out. I mean, it completely ruined what he had planned, but maybe it was meant to be in the moment. It made it more memorable, I suppose. It makes me laugh even now, all these years on.

At the time, with the ring, and being young, on holiday, I remember I was excited.

But further into the relationship, there were some cracks that started to appear.

I'm quite a free spirit, shall we say, and being independent it was perhaps more apparent to me that I was being somewhat suffocated by my lack of personal time. Looking back, sadly it was those signs that concerned me at the very beginning, and I should have trusted my intuition more. I did air my concerns about how intense the relationship felt, but Andrew was incredibly charming and would go all out to woo and impress me so I pushed my niggles aside as just nerves.

Andrew was all about cameras, angles, etc., and that translated into a love of taking endless photos of everything, including the two of us together. It started to feel akin to those sorts of people who stereotypically post endless photos, smiling on Instagram, to hide their real lives. It made me feel that our relationship was based very much around our image and presenting as a perfect couple.

My mum wouldn't give the pages of photos the time and attention. I used to see her looking at them all and the facial expressions alone were a bit of a giveaway. She was never one to hold back with her thoughts anyway! Ay, Mum?

I felt like I was being put on a pedestal, which is ridiculous as it forced me to try to live up to his expectations, and that's not healthy.

We started to argue more and more, until it became tit for tat really, and then, of course, the writing was on the wall. When I told him the pressure was too much, he'd rein it in a bit and would try to patch over the cracks.

All in all, it was extremely difficult, exhausting and draining for both of us, especially while we were trying to give our best performances at work on a daily basis.

It was drawn out over almost an entire year, but eventually we made the decision to end things.

Afterwards, I moved out of London, away from acting to recharge my batteries with a holiday.

No more men, I thought, as I mapped out my exciting first months as a newly single, free woman. I am done. But they do say when you stop chasing something then it comes to you . . .

After *Primeval* had ended and I'd split from Andrew, I was delivered just the medicine I needed with a role in *One Man, Two Guvnors*.

It was a massive show that had launched with James Corden as the hugely funny lead character. The fast-paced comedy was a hit in the West End and on Broadway, and I went into the second cast of the London version after James had left.

The audience's constant belly laughing was the tonic I needed, as it lifts and carries you along. You keep laughing with them. That's the way the play was set up, with full-on comedy from start to finish.

I did it for eight months, and it was a great thing to be involved with; it got me through a really difficult patch.

Following on from *One Man, Two Guvnors*, I landed some lovely acting jobs including recurring parts in *Casualty* and *EastEnders*.

In *Casualty* I played a devious, hard-up woman called Mercedes Christie and my opening scene sees her mug a guy and get a massive piece of wood and whack a man around the head.

Being the new girl in an established show as big as *Casualty*, I was initially apprehensive about whether the cast would take to me, but they really welcomed me and it was one of the nicest sets I've ever worked on. The cast were lovely on the show. But it was an unfortunate time for me as it coincided with a decline in my health.

It was a thrill to be on *EastEnders* in 2017 as I've watched it all my life, and my parents are addicted to it. Regardless of what else was on, at my parents' house, *EastEnders* is never missed. To go into the Queen Vic and walk around the set was rather magical. It's strange when you see the actual set because it looks so different in real life from how it looks on telly.

A lot of the characters from my days as a viewer had moved on, but a few of the original legends still remain, and I got to meet some of them which was very exciting stuff.

I knew Linda behind the bar, because Kellie Bright, who plays her, was Andrew's sister's best friend.

I also knew Danny Dyer a little bit, as he used to come around to our flat in north London to see me, Paul, Neil and Sheridan. I think his daughter Dani's brilliant. His adult daughter! Funny how time flies . . . I thought she was great on *Love Island*.

Dean Gaffney, who I knew from my youth, also welcomed me with open arms and he seemed to have matured so much (more than me maybe! Hehe) and levelled out from our wild days.

It's amazing to be involved with something like *EastEnders*. It might seem like a glamorous job but boy do they graft on a daily basis! It's a very intense schedule and there's so much to fit in due to the number of screenings per week. You're constantly learning new lines. And I take forever learning lines (it's a work in progress), but the regular cast do it so well.

The set is friendly but reserved. In fairness I think because most people are regular – some having been working there for decades – it's got that established feel to it where they don't socialise as much after filming, unlike *Primeval*, where we were such a social team. *Primeval* was more like a film set as it was always a different location and we were travelling, so there was a sense of adventure.

On *EastEnders*, everyone has to go straight home to learn their lines so they can work the next day and keep up that fast-paced schedule. It doesn't leave room for going out on the town.

What I also found difficult is the fewer number of takes that you get for each scene; it's certainly not unlimited takes because there's such a tight schedule and so that knowledge carries different pressures. And coming from a show that was made like a film, so you'd take your time, get all your angles, and keep doing it until it was perfect, I had to be READY!

In *EastEnders*, there are three cameras set up in a room, and you'd get pretty much the whole scene done in a few takes before moving on. There might be different set-ups for some scenes, but just not to the degree that I was used to. It was certainly a big adjustment from what felt like 'unlimited takes'.

I have done a couple of projects since then, just to keep a toe dipped in the water, but I have turned down just about everything I've been offered. That's mainly because if I do something, it'll have to be something I absolutely love, to keep me away from the family for any length of time.

© BBC Archive

I spent months preparing to get knocked about in the ring for this Sport Relief match. I'm ready for a rematch any time you like!

I actually don't remeber this boat or where we were going,
but I really like this picture of me and Paul.

Me and Paul enjoying life!

Passing the time, waiting for
the après ski, up the Matterhorn
in Zermatt, Switzerland.

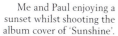

Me and Paul enjoying a
sunset whilst shooting the
album cover of 'Sunshine'.

On set of S1 Ep2 of *Primeval*. We used tennis balls to measure the eye-line of the dinosaurs.

Can't forget the elephants or James Murray! Just a casual day in the life on the set of *Primeval*.

Me and my costar, Lucy Brown who played Claudia, wasting time while waiting to shoot our next scene.

Me as Pauline, being over-dramatic opposite Gemma Whelan in *One Man, Two Guvnors*. This production was at the Theatre Royal Haymarket in the West End.

© BBC Archive

My character, Kandice Taylor and Bernie in the famous *Eastenders* cafe.

© BBC Archive

My character, Mercedes in *Casualty*. No makeup needed!

Tora and me in Gran Canaria, Spain.

Ready to go 'out out' in Gran Canaria.

With Leah and a friend at the opening of *The Walking Dead* ride in Thorpe Park.

Pretty in pink!

Tora decorating . . .
(herself, for a change!)

Adam and I holding down the fort at W6 Gym.

I wasn't born with an incredible voice, and have to work a lot harder than other singers. I just lack confidence in my singing ability, I guess, and that doesn't help either.

My dad thinks I'm a wonderful singer, but he may need his hearing tested. I'm not saying singing is out of bounds completely, but I'm always the one at the back, doing the harmonies and stuff like that. I can stay in tune, but it's not a lead-vocals voice. And that's why it was very easy for me to know that being a pop singer wasn't my calling – and why I tend to run when offered singing-heavy musical roles!

Because truly, we all want to do something that we're talented or good at. Obviously practising hard at something is no issue if you've got that passion and that talent to begin with.

But honestly, I have tried and tried with singing, and it's not *terrible*, but my voice is nothing special. It's just limited; I'm under no illusions that I am Whitney Houston.

However, film and TV series I wouldn't mind another crack at the right role. I've learned so much since my early days, and it would be nice to translate those skills into something I can get my teeth into.

Unfortunately, it is a very difficult world to integrate with a family life, and you can't do it unless you're fully committed. But now the girls aren't babies anymore, I think it would be a lot more manageable. And I do keep planning to get myself an acting agent as I haven't had one in ages – so watch this space.

Even though the S Club TV series were reality TV of a kind, I have turned down several offers to do reality shows in the years since. Watching what happened to Jo in *Celebrity Big Brother* put me off for life, as it affected her for so many years afterwards and did real damage to her. It seemed like she just didn't want to be there, and the rest is history.

I think maybe there was a naivety at the beginning of reality TV where you could say what you wanted, without a second thought, and not be held accountable. I have no comment on the *Big Brother* incident. I will say that my personal experience, unrelated to *Big Brother*, is that since the day I met Jo, I've never heard a racist remark come out of her mouth.

As I said, Jo really suffered, and after the show she plunged to a very dark place with her mental health, and spoke in the press about having suicidal thoughts. Seeing how somebody as strong as Jo could be brought down in such a cruel way was horrible to watch, and I was very worried about her. Every day she wishes she had never, ever set foot in that house, and I don't blame her. I often wonder, do the press want people to recognise the error of their ways and apologise, or push them to the brink of topping themselves? Because I've yet to see the former.

These days, I might consider *I'm a Celebrity ... Get Me Out of Here!* Let's be honest, it's probably the biggest reality TV show and yes, arguably the most difficult, but that's the appeal.

Not that many years ago I had a couple of auditions for *Dancing on Ice* – which Rachel did recently – but then I got pregnant so I never got the chance, and then Covid came. It's quite something when you're swung round, your head an inch away from the ice! Who knows, maybe one day!

Chapter Eleven

Storm in a B Cup

S ome of the things that you're about to read about happened to me, not twenty-five years ago, but in the last
three or so years.

Health for me was something that I took for granted in
my earlier years. However, later in life it is something that I
wanted to make my career, away from being in a band, away
from being an actress in films or being on stage in whatever
show. It's not that I didn't enjoy those experiences – because
many of them I didn't just enjoy, I loved – but I knew that
long-term health, nutrition, wellbeing and looking after
people with the love of my life alongside me was probably
my true calling.

I could envision being a mother, a partner, a business-
woman and a gym instructor. Basically, somebody who people
could turn to, who had an abundance of life experience (some
good, some not so good), and would help them in their journey to better health. Sounds idyllic, doesn't it? Well, that's
rewind those three years and actually see how it played out
in the real world of Hannah Spearritt.

A few months into my new relationship with Adam I made
what I now think was the worst mistake of my life.

I got breast implants.

I'd been thinking about having them done for about ten years. In my early twenties I'd gone for a consultation, but didn't do anything about it further.

In school I wasn't overly body conscious as I was so unbelievably sporty and a dancer – no ballerina wants boobs. Boobs would have been a hindrance.

I do remember hearing boys commenting on a girl's body one day. I remember thinking, *God, what do bodies even matter?* So as a teenager I was never really aware of not having big boobs, and didn't really know if they were going to develop.

I guess when I got into S Club 7 and was thrown into doing a lot of magazine and video shoots and stuff like that, it put the spotlight on me and made me body conscious. You can pull better shapes dancing if you've got a bit of curve.

To be clear: I was never told I had to get a boob job by the recording company, but curvier models were being portrayed as sexy in the media – people like Kelly Brook, Katie Price and Abbey Clancy – that's what was selling, popular and seen as more attractive. There was negative chat around the skinny girl, or whatever you may call it. If I'm to remember rightly, and I might remember wrongly, I don't know, but I don't ever remember my body shape being celebrated.

Kate Moss's waif look had fallen out of favour, and I was impressionable and susceptible to outside influences. Things were starting to get into my subconscious of what was attractive and beautiful.

On lads' mags shoots, the photographers didn't say anything. But, as you can imagine, when you had to do a shoot like that, there's a lot of wardrobe available and lots of bikinis and underwear.

And I couldn't help but compare myself to Rachel, Jo, and Tina who all were beautiful and had amazing boobs. Sheridan had great boobs as well. I was just surrounded by great boobs. It's not their fault, and it wasn't a jealousy thing. But that is essentially what I was surrounded by, and so I guess when we did photo shoots where there was a lot of focus on our bodies underneath the clothes, I started to want larger tits.

And I was very young when I started doing those shoots. I probably wasn't fully developed. That's not to say I grew into a huge chest, but there was that element to it then as well. The other women in the band were all that little bit older, and their boobs had had time to grow, which threw even more of a spotlight on my own body.

And it was just something I didn't ever really want my focus on. But I started to blame myself for not being a stronger character who should have been able to deal with it. When you are doing photo shoots, the focus is entirely on the front of your body, and the size of your chest and that's a weird and unhealthy way to spend a day.

I never felt unconfident with my face or any other aspect of my body, so I vowed to try to make the most of them and used these gel fillers inside my bra, which were becoming popular at that time. I didn't feel comfortable without any padding, so I would come prepared with my little fillers because I felt too conscious to be in front of a camera without anything.

But then I just got fed up with putting them in.

One flew out once when dancing in a club – not on the

stage during a live performance, thank goodness (can you imagine that?!) – but I was still so embarrassed.

A girl came across and said, 'Hi, is this your . . . ' and I'm like, 'Oh, yep, sorry.' You try to pretend you're fine and can laugh about it, but you take it all on board all the same.

So when it became a thing that people were getting their boobs done and it was an option, I started to think that maybe it could be the answer.

I wasn't that self-conscious in that area that it actually stopped me getting closer to boys, but I did worry at the thought of one ever finding a gel filler tucked into my bra.

I remember seeing Katie Price while we were doing a photo shoot, and she was getting dressed – swapping her costume for a T-shirt. The costume came off, the bra came off, and the T-shirt went on. I saw the famous KP boobs – this was before she'd had surgery – in all their naked glory in the mirror, and gasped.

She was so stunning, the ultimate jaw-dropping pin-up, and I looked down at my chest and laughed.

Being in the band there was a pressure to look a certain way. I mean, we spent hours over the course of the day going back to make sure everything – hair, make-up, tits and teeth – was perfect.

Again, it was just all about the exterior and as a result there was a huge amount of pressure in terms of what we looked like – after all, that was a massive part of why we were initially picked.

Looking back, I don't know if anybody was able to see how uncomfortable I was, because I got used to wearing a very good mask. It didn't seem like it was something I could or should speak to anyone about – or that they could help with. Those weren't the sort of conversations we would have. And that could have been my fault because the mask I put on each day to get through it got so good.

I don't know. And maybe they didn't expect anything, which is a shame because it would've been nice to be in a position where we did speak about things that were bothering us slightly, or at least feel like we could be more honest with each other.

And the longer I went without talking about it, the more difficult it got and the more it was affecting my life – but I still never brought it up.

In the early days it must not have bothered me. I watched back *Miami 7* recently and saw myself playing volleyball; I didn't have any padding on there, and it's nice to see that freedom and realise that I obviously wasn't thinking about it then.

I was eighteen then, and flat as a pancake, but I was wearing a bikini without a care in the world. It only began to affect me after I did the first lads' mag and they airbrushed my body to give me more curves.

I do sometimes question if I'd have been so fixated on the size of my breasts had I not worked in this showbiz world, and it's really difficult to say for sure. But I don't think so. If I was to imagine myself having taken a different route in life, I can't imagine it would have been as much of an issue.

Before going for the surgery consultation, I opened up to Mum and had a conversation with her about it, explaining to her that I wasn't happy.

She was surprised to hear that I was feeling down, and how

it was affecting my confidence. And as it would be for any mother, it was really sad for her to hear that something like that would be getting in the way of all the good stuff I had going on and everything I had to be grateful for.

I ended up having that conversation with her, explaining that so many women were getting this procedure now without having any problems, and that I thought it was going to make my life easier.

My poor mum. Now, as a mother myself, I can't even imagine what it would feel like to have your daughter say that to you. But she was very supportive and open-minded when she realised in the moment how long I'd be thinking about it for.

The reason I didn't jump into surgery the first time I had a consultation was that I just wasn't sure it was right. But the idea of it lingered and I kept returning to that unhealthy mentality of thinking they could be more perfect and focusing on what I didn't have rather than what I had.

But as breast implants were becoming so popular and common, there hadn't really been any sort of bad press about them (apart from the PIP controversy, but those types of implants weren't on the market anymore) and there seemed to be a lot of women out there that were happy with the results.

And so it just seemed like an option worth considering because it was still affecting my life and I was sort of boring myself a bit, thinking every time I got dressed about how I could look fuller in the bust if I got implants.

I was talking to my therapist during the last leg of my relationship with Andrew, and she gave me the details of her surgeon. Thinking back, a therapist giving me her plastic surgeon's details seems about as ethically wrong as you can get but I didn't think twice at the time, which is a reminder of how my priorities were completely wrong back then. I went along for a consultation and the relationship with Andrew broke down shortly afterwards. I do remember thinking, well once I was single again that maybe this is the right time, just to give myself a little bit of a pick-me-up boost, but I didn't follow through until I'd started going out with Adam. I saved that shit show all for him, the lucky guy!

He tried his hardest to stop me. Why the fuck did I not listen? What an absolute twat!

Hindsight is a wonderful thing, isn't it? But maybe I needed to go through a tragic or terrible ordeal to wake up from my drunk-on-fame stupor, shall we call it? Nobody would ever wish for ill health, but it does make you appreciative of the days when you are well. Maybe if I'd not had the surgery I would have done other things that would have caused me to burn out quicker – you just never know.

Nevertheless, it's been a hard learning path – my thirties were wiped out as a result – and six months after getting it done, I was gone. I had been so fit at the time.

It was weird because we didn't know what was happening, and the most difficult part was not being believed along the journey because we didn't really know what was going on ourselves. Trying to work it out was the most difficult thing because it wasn't something that could be diagnosed.

All we knew was that I'd had a great bill of health going into the surgery, and I didn't recover well.

I should have healed a bit quicker. But then my health declined rapidly. I started getting every symptom under the sun, and even my personality changed. I was put on so many different drugs. When I look back on that time, I just don't recognise myself.

About a week before the operation, on 20 August 2013, I told Adam that I was booked to have breast implant surgery.

He came with me to meet the surgeon. He thought the doctor was a 'polished' salesman and had some other thoughts I won't share here, which turned out to be right in the end.

The surgeon showed me the implant, which was called a cohesive teardrop, explaining that it looked really natural and that if you cut it no liquid would come out. The implant was also a textured one, which helped it to not swivel all day as the round shaped ones are liable to do. He described it as a jelly bean that wouldn't go anywhere. But what he didn't say was that essentially it was still packed with chemicals, and they could sweat out into your system.

What's more, the texture of the implant – designed to grip more to the breast tissue – means that it's a lot easier for mould to attach and grow on the surface AND they contain even more chemicals. So, I had the perfect combination to make it the implant with the largest potential to damage my health. But it obviously wasn't sold to me in that way.

And my surgeon made me feel confident that he was good at what he does, and I believed him. His record spoke for itself.

I went for a B cup. I didn't want to go for anything bigger that would be disproportionate to my body. I just wanted to fill the bra of the size that I naturally am, which is a 32B.

I later discovered that after children your body changes naturally and I could end up with much bigger breasts. Mum told me, 'I never had boobs when I was your age until after I had children. You'll probably be the same.'

I confess that somewhere in the back of my mind was a niggly doubt about whether this was the right thing to do as I signed on the bottom line and handed over £7,000.

I asked him again if it was OK, and he assured me my recovery would be straightforward. I never could have imagined it would take quite as long as it did.

To anyone thinking about having it done, it is your body, it is your choice. But please do think really carefully, because the recuperation time can be much longer than they tell you, as can the potential side effects.

On the day of my surgery, I went in early to the hospital and didn't have any thoughts of running out of the door. Registration was a straightforward process, and I was quickly taken down to the operating theatre. I remember being given a blue gown and seeing someone getting the anaesthetic ready, and then a woman came over to me and reassured me that it would be all right.

Then it started to feel real and I remember thinking, *Shit, I don't want to wake up and find my body different to the point that I don't recognise myself.*

So then, lying on the bed, I started having all these weird doubts and fears, but they started to administer the anaesthetic and – boom! – I was out.

When I came around from surgery I felt really groggy, swollen and ill, and just wanted Adam by my side.

He had dropped me off at the hospital and had tried again to get me to change my mind before going into surgery but to no avail unfortunately. We'd been together for such a short time, so it was an enormous pressure to put on our relationship. He made it extremely clear to me that he thought it was a stupid thing to do. And that was *before* it made me sick.

I texted him to say I was out now if he wanted to come and say hello.

When he arrived I think he got a shock looking at me. I had drains in my chest with all the fluid coming out from the operation and it was all self-inflicted, cringe.

I was excited but a little bit fearful looking down at my bandaged chest, and surprised to see how high up the chest wall the implants were positioned. I couldn't see over them when I was lying down, due to the swelling, and it was like having two camel humps stuck on my chest. My body seemed completely different. Everything felt so much bigger around my torso, and I was slightly concerned that the surgeon had put in much bigger implants than I had requested.

The surgeon popped into the room and allayed all my fears with assurances that they'd go down and settle, and that they do sit higher initially.

In those first forty-eight hours your body forms a capsule around the implant to protect itself and that triggered my immune system to go into overdrive; that's what caused all the trouble.

Adam says that if he'd known about the risks at the time, then we'd have fallen out about it, a hundred per cent. But he also points out that I probably wouldn't have had the operation done if I'd known the risk that it carried, regardless of how much I wanted it. And he's right. That's why we made the documentary – *Me & My Breast Implants* – because they don't tell women that it's a possibility that your body can react like it did.

I followed the protocol for the first six weeks: no driving, no lifting (not that I could do any of that anyway). Adam had to help dress me some days because I couldn't lift my arms over my head.

What concerned both of us was that it was taking longer than we expected to get back to normal. The surgeon had said it was normal, that they would drop down in a few months and look more natural.

Well, they never did settle down. They stayed unnaturally high on the chest wall. I didn't mind them in a bra but they didn't look good out of one, and they certainly didn't look like what I'd asked for.

I tried to accept it, and two months after the operation I started to get back into exercising with Adam. We signed up to do a hundred-mile bike ride to Brighton in June 2014, but my ill health became apparent after the event.

Adam and I would train in the morning early and he noticed I was having to come back and sleep, which was not something that I'd experienced before. Usually I feel very energised after exercise, especially as I was in the best physical shape of my life prior to the surgery. We were doing hill sprints three days a week, weights in the gym and going on bike rides together a lot, as well as eating very well – eliminating caffeine and gluten.

And then one day I needed a nap, and after that I needed a nap every day. It went from one hour to three hours, and got longer and longer and longer, to the point where I was asleep more than I was awake.

I'd wake up, have an unbelievably bad panic attack, and go back to bed again.

And it just absolutely floored me.

My body was not responding well to the extra exercise, and I was having panic attacks out of nowhere, despite never having suffered with them before. And obviously that drains your energy. Adam had seen that pre-surgery, my fitness level was easily good enough to do that bike ride. So he didn't really understand what was wrong at first.

He said I was manic for the whole trip, and it didn't make sense that I'd gone from being OK to completely losing it, my health completely gone, in the space of two months.

By September I couldn't really leave the house. I was sleeping all day. I continued to have panic attacks and my hair was falling out. My ears were ringing from tinnitus and then there were dreadful visual disturbances.

Things became so bad just before Casualty, we had to set my bedroom up on the ground floor and I moved downstairs because I couldn't walk up the stairs anymore. Adam often had to help me physically get around; at my lowest ebb he had to carry me.

I'm very good at covering up what's going on. So people never knew how bad it was.

I hate to worry people and unless my mum needs to know something, I will always try and deal with it myself, and try not to worry her.

What's more, in the state I was in, I wasn't up for a conversation or anything like that, so my parents didn't know how bad things had got. When they came to visit at Christmas, they didn't really understand what was wrong as the symptoms didn't really tally up with any common conditions – they just wondered why I was fast asleep most of the day when they'd come to see me from Gorleston. Adam helped me through onto the couch to lie down, and then I just passed out in front of them, asleep. I didn't wake up for hours.

At this point, Adam and I decided enough was enough. I had to try and see a doctor who could help, and so we made appointments with top consultants from almost every medical discipline.

And they all said the same thing: it was not the implants causing my symptoms. It was all in my head.

Adam always says that, knowing what we know now, and how we were continuously lied to, from an ethical perspective, the doctors we saw are – in his personal opinion – a disgrace to the medical profession.

Each consultation was costing around two grand, and included multiple tests. All of them ended up referring me to a psychiatrist because they didn't know what was going on. Perhaps it should have been the other way around!

We saw one immunologist, apparently a top one in the UK. He sarcastically laughed at Adam when Adam told him that he was 99% sure it was the implants.

Adam lost his temper at that particular consultant, saying, 'Look at her, she's like the living dead!'

But he ignored Adam and muttered, 'No, it's all in your head', even though Adam had practically carried me in.

Another consultant we'd pinned our hopes on scoffed at the idea that it could be the breast implants causing my extreme immune response – and this was after he'd watched me, white as a sheet, be near on carried into his room.

By and large, the studies on breast implant illness are carried out by the silicone implant manufacturers, and so they take the results to the doctors and that provides the doctors with enough evidence to suggest there is no evidence of breast implant illness. Then they tell anyone that comes to them with symptoms that they can't be caused by the implants – it's got to be something else. And that's their watertight argument. That is the opinion of the doctors who treat breast implant illness.

But the doctors we spoke to just did not want to deviate from that hymn sheet or entertain the idea of implants causing these problems.

Adam spent months researching, and we found one doctor in Twickenham, funnily enough, who was prepared to brainstorm with us. Dr Manreet Johal will always have a special place in our hearts because he really cares about his patients. He has an open mind and he is amazing. From the bottom of our hearts, thank you so much. In the end, he was the only one that helped with my symptoms. And he was prepared to try anything. He would let us do our own research and present it to him.

I found out there was a two-year warranty on the implants. Two years for something that will live in your body for the recommended ten-year minimum lifespan.

We called back the surgeon who did my surgery after nineteen months, and Adam told him that I was very sick: 'She's had a clean bill of health her whole life, and now she's sick. The only thing that fits is the breast implants, and she has a two-year warranty, so can you please take them out?'

You know what he told us?

He flatly said: 'No.'

Adam could tell, as soon as the conversation had started, that he was clearly asking qualifying questions to make sure he had no liability. That was his main concern – he couldn't give a shit about my health, just didn't want to be liable for the explant, which we now know would've immediately restored the majority of my health. And, interestingly enough, he denied that breast implants had ever caused any illness, and started stating details of this study and that. Well then, he would know that breast implants have in fact killed many women over the years and made countless more terribly sick. Lovely guy.

He explained that they would only take them out in the case of certain, specific complications.

They basically have a watertight warranty for themselves, not the patient, which ensures that they'll never have to remove anything – and this guy was a very senior, reputable surgeon.

It's not like I went to some cheap backstreet clinic. It's an absolute disgrace. The medical world is like the Wild West.

Around then, I got the call to audition for Casualty. Looking back, I have no idea how I got the role, considering how sick I was. The one saving grace was the fact that my character was a drug addict, so she looked sick all the time anyway! I could sort of get away with looking pale, and like death.

I had nothing. No energy, no life, and I was suffering with so many symptoms. It felt like I was dead inside, like a zombie.

I was so pleased to be joining the show, and Adam said he would help support me through it, driving to and from the studios in Cardiff – but we had no idea how bad things were going to get.

I cannot remember any of those car journeys; I had eyes, but the world was passing me by.

Trying to act on Casualty became a living nightmare. We would drive from London to Cardiff and then I would sleep the entire day and have four espressos so that I had enough energy to perform in an hour-long shoot.

During my time on the show, my health deteriorated severely. I would come through the door of the dressing room and pass out again. Adam would wait for another hour or two and then drive me back either to the hotel or home.

Trying to learn my lines was another nightmare. We'd sit in bed going over the same one scene, of just a few lines, and that would take us maybe nine or ten hours – the whole day – to learn. In that time, Adam would learn three other people's parts from the script so he knew when to prompt me and to keep me on track.

One day there was literally just one word I had to say, and I couldn't get it. It was so embarrassing. I wanted the floor to swallow me up. Adam was scared of what was happening to me.

I think some of the cast and crew on Casualty must have wondered if I was a drug addict or something, given my exhaustive, dead-behind-the-eyes state.

When I was making my television documentary, I visited a director from Casualty. He gave a hilarious – in my eyes – account of my breakdown over the course of my three-month contract. Basically there was a lot of chat backstage about what kind of drugs I was on.

It didn't help that to control the pain I had been prescribed a really strong drug called pregabalin, which is normally given for extreme anxiety and after amputations. It basically desensitises the nerves so that you can't feel any pain; it's also used for epilepsy but it's a very strong anti-anxiety drug.

It was prescribed ahead of the S Club reunion tour in April 2015 in the hope that if I couldn't feel anything then I could carry on working. And it worked at first, getting me from being bedridden to having a spring in my step. It got me through the tour, but I kept taking it and eventually the efficacy waned. In the meantime, I'd done a lot more damage to my insides by pushing my body when it was screaming in pain.

Adam was living in fear of me crashing and not recovering because as I said, pregabalin desensitises the nerve endings. It deadened me inside and changed me into somebody else. It felt like I was trying to fight a battle that I could never win because there was a toxic load being put into my body by the silicone on a daily basis.

As well as the autoimmune disease I suffered with, these implants have also been linked to a rare cancer called BIA-ALCL (Breast Implant Associated Anaplastic Large Cell Lymphoma): a specific cancer that's only caused by breast implants.

As soon as the implant is removed, the cancer stops, because the root cause has been taken away – it's damning evidence.

We didn't try to sue because of the amount of trauma it caused. We didn't have the energy or time to compile a class-action lawsuit as it would've robbed us of our time and our days would have been full of even more misery and negative shit, and we'd had enough of that already.

So we said, *look, let's just forget about it and try and move on.* It's difficult because you do want to hold people accountable, but at the same time, you know you've got to choose your battles. I am still angry about it. There is still anger in me. Definitely.

While I was ill, Adam set up a Facebook group and we received thousands of messages from women all over the world, telling me the most heart-breaking stories that you could ever imagine.

Adam and I couldn't respond to the messages anymore because it was such a commitment, and it was so sad hearing things like, 'I've got three kids and I got my implant when the third one was three years old. And I've missed their whole childhood being in bed for the last ten years.'

There were so many stories like that, and the running theme was, 'I can't afford to get them taken out'. Most women in this position are so ill, and yet they can't afford to have the implants taken out to get better, which is one of the heart-breaking aspects to it.

Prior to the documentary and writing this book, I avoided talking about it. And I guess I now feel that I've made my peace with it, but it's still a subject that hurts because I know they're still destroying women's lives.

We suffered for so long, for so many years, and we lost so much from it – financially as well as in every other respect. I just feel that I can't waste any more of my life dwelling on it.

In total, adding up all the doctors' fees, consultations, tests, travel to various clinics and hospitals, therapists and the cost to remove the implants, I spent more than £100,000.

So the money I made from the 2015 reunion tour concerts was spent almost entirely on that. What a monumental waste of money.

The pressure and trauma of what I was enduring put my and Adam's relationship under the most enormous strain. Adam almost stopped seeing me as his girlfriend, but rather as a patient to be cared for.

It became hard to tell what was really me and what was the illness. The lines were so blurred, and half the time we were so stressed out of our minds that we didn't know what was going on.

It was really sad for him as he only had a few months of getting to know me before I had the implants inserted. I told him, 'This isn't fair on you – you need to go, as I can't give myself to a relationship right now.'

But at the same time, I couldn't afford to not have him there because I couldn't actually look after myself.

But I was very difficult to live with in the early days – no, years – of our relationship. I was pushing him away as I just couldn't bear being unwell. I'm a terrible patient.

It had a terrible impact on our intimacy as well because I was aware of looking so, so ill and didn't ever feel attractive whilst I was ill. In fact for Adam, it was probably like cuddling a corpse I imagine, I was so thin and frail at times.

They say that you get the experiences that you need in life. Well, we certainly learned a lot from the process. Although it was horrific, I do now care more about other people and a lot less about myself. And I think it changed us hugely.

In 2016 I had the implants removed by a different doctor, Dr McDiarmid. He said that most women – nine out of ten – get better after they get them removed. He was recommended to me by a doctor in Dallas, who we spoke to in our documentary. He was the first doctor to tell me,'there is no test', and 'if you're sick it's almost definitely the implants but you can never be 100% until they're removed'.

When I woke up after the removal surgery I felt almost like myself again. I did feel a lot better instantly.

Upon waking up, I could tell that my body was really happy, almost like it was saying thank you. It wasn't having to fight anymore. Some symptoms disappeared straight away: I always had a low-grade fever, and that had gone, and I think my energy levels were a lot higher.

We went out for a meal on the way back home from the surgery, which was exciting – the last time we had done that was before the implants were put in.

The visual disturbances I was getting had gone and there was just a sense of wellbeing in my body rather than what I had been feeling. It was quite the dramatic improvement.

But I have had lasting problems from the autoimmune disease – bouts of exhaustion that sometimes stop me playing with full energy with my children, and I am angry at myself because I feel it was my fault for having the surgery in the first place.

Given what's happened to my body, I swerve injectables and facelifts, choosing to age gracefully. It would be really stupid to risk my immune system with Botox, fillers or threads. I do fear the damage those quick fixtures could potentially cause women.

They're not for me anyway, even if they were totally safe, I think I'd still prefer to keep some character in my face with a few wrinkles!

I've followed the anti-Candida diet, because it was the only diet that improved the symptoms of breast implant illness. It's really strict and it wasn't easy, but my body definitely liked it.

I also much prefer how my breasts look now, and having children made them look fuller and better.

Weirdly, it's almost like the implant had stretched them and made them look bigger anyway. Maybe it altered the shape of where the muscle sits, and made them look a bit more prominent.

I did breastfeed my girls for a little bit, but I wrestled with what was the right thing to do as I was concerned there might still be chemicals in my breast tissue that could contaminate my breast milk.

Those horrible years could have driven me to suicide, and while I never planned to kill myself, Adam will tell you there were days when I would say I didn't think I could carry on, or question what the point was if I was never going to recover from this.

It was upsetting for him to hear me express these thoughts, and he felt crippled with anxiety leaving me alone sometimes when he had to go to work.

So when I first started to take the pregabalin to get me through the tour it was like it made me feel alive again, because I hadn't been able to work for a long time at that point.

I'd been bedridden for so long that I'd have taken anything if it promised to get me back on my feet and walking again.

And when I could dance, the euphoria I felt was incredible, because I hadn't felt that freedom since getting ill.

Up to the start of the reunion tour, none of the band knew the extent of what was going on. They were aware of something being up because they knew I had all these dietary requirements and I looked really ill on these tablets, but again I didn't care about cosmetic side effects because all I knew was that something was making me feel better; I was willing to take that short term gain regardless of the damage it was going to do to me long term.

And I had been in such a dark place that I was willing to do anything to escape. So I did speak to them about it, but I didn't want to go into too much detail – I wanted to forget.

Essentially, I was running away from how bad things were and just using whatever I could to get some energy. In the back of my mind I always knew that I'd have to crash back into the reality of what was going on in my body, because it was false energy and it couldn't last long.

We were only on tour for about a month, but I knew I had to come off them as soon as the tour was over.

There were moments in this period I'm not proud of. I hurt people around me. There are things I did I am ashamed of because my actions caused pain, and I am disappointed in the way I handled stuff.

I wasn't facing up to things, instead throwing spurious reasons for escaping because I was so desperate to feel alive again. So I pushed Adam away because he was a constant reminder of my illness.

Paul and I got close again on that tour – we were always drawn to each other – and it was a bit fucked up. I just didn't know what I was doing. And I suppose because he knew the younger me as well, and he knew me when I was well, I was being selfish and using him to make myself feel young and pretend to be well again. We just sort of started connecting in the same way that we always had.

I didn't plan to go back to him, and I am working on trying to forgive myself, but I just wanted to feel carefree and young. I thought that Paul would fix my illness and take the pain away.

But I wasn't thinking about anyone else in the process and was lashing out.

How do you get your head around these times? I still struggle with that, I suppose, because I've had quite a lot of them where I've been mentally unwell and acted out.

After the tour, Paul and I fizzled out quite quickly. It was just as it had been the first time: when we were in the schedule of work, the S Club machine, things between us kind of worked. But afterwards they stopped working.

I immediately regretted it because I'd hurt Adam and missed him a lot.

But in a funny sort of way, I guess it gave me and Paul some closure. It hadn't really ended that amicably the first time round. There was still stuff that I don't think either of us had thought through probably, and I think we resolved that in 2015.

It's all about growing together, isn't it? And just realising that it was never really meant to be, I guess, but I probably regret it for Paul's sake. I think it might have hurt him, even though he also came to the conclusion that we weren't right together.

I couldn't help but yearn for Adam, who was such a different man, with a completely different energy that I love, and a caring, nurturing, loving nature.

I'd lost my way at the time, so it wasn't fair to bring anyone else into that.

And I didn't even fancy him when I saw him. It was familiarity and an energy connection, I guess. But it just wasn't quite there for either of us the second time around.

We had some conversations in a cafe, and I was heartened when our make-up artist told me how he'd started out shy and blossomed over the tour, which was quite sweet.

He was gaining confidence and he was gaining momentum with becoming Paul again.

It was really lovely to watch, and we all had a good time. I just wanted to get him on the right track. And that sounds ridiculous, because he was his own man and he goes at his own speed. But even though I was completely messed up myself, I just felt like I could help a bit with agents and stuff and get him a show.

In fact, I did. I put him in touch with an agent I know and he got a part in a tour of *The Rocky Horror Show*.

I just wanted him to be okay, but sadly we probably fucked each other up more in the process.

And even though he was older than me, by the second time we got together, I had more life experience behind me and that probably gave me more confidence in being assertive with my life choices.

I wasn't really expecting anything. I think I just found the whole coming back together thing quite interesting because we were so many years on from our old selves. I needed to find out if it would work, having had all those intervening years of growth. And if we weren't right together now, then I guess it was never meant to be.

I was so messed up, and I can't even say that I was more confident, but I probably convinced *myself* I was more confident. I felt like at least I was portraying a confident image.

But it got messy very quickly after the tour.

Paul came back to my house, and we'd taken this picture of the two of us smiling in the sunshine. Adam saw the photo come up on an iPad we shared, and so it all got a little bit confrontational. Adam made his presence known, Paul left, and I didn't really hear from him after that, which was a little bit difficult for me to understand, if I'm honest.

Adam and I were apart for some time after that. Things were really inflamed over the next few months and because of all this medication that I had been on, chat about me being under the influence had got back to my agent.

He was concerned that I was drinking heavily (he didn't know about the meds) and called my dad. Everything came out about the painkillers, and it was decided I had to be sent to rehab because by this point I was clearly struggling to get off the medication.

It's really difficult to come off such a powerful painkiller. If you stop taking it too quickly you can go into seizures, which is scary, so you have to gradually reduce your intake, which leaves you in a feverish state.

I tried to go cold turkey at one stage, which wasn't wise.

But when I got sent to rehab, I thought it was going to be a great opportunity for me to get off this medication. I could use it for that, even though my agent thought my problem was with alcohol (and probably illegal drugs or whatever), but what I didn't realise was that they keep you on your medication so things don't change. And you just talk about the trauma of what you've gone through. And I was like, Oh God, I've been here for a month now and I'm on the same medication which is the issue.

I did try to tell them. And the staff told me we had to deal with the trauma and the psychological stuff before we started changing the medication.

There were no other celebrities there. We would get up and set our goal of the day, set out our intention for the day. It was a nice small group of people, in a lovely house with gorgeous gardens. We would start each day with an hour of therapy, followed by morning medication, which was diazepam, just to relax us. Then we'd go into group therapy, all sat around in a room, and then different sessions of different things – there might be a bit of yoga in the afternoon, or some sessions you'd do in the garden just to mix it up. But it was all really chilled and therapy-based.

And we had quite a few breaks and got to know people there. Everyone would gather round the little smokers' corner. I hadn't smoked for years, and I started smoking because of rehab! Along with a new daily dose of diazepam! A place where people are sent to break addictions. You couldn't make it up, but that's where everyone used to congregate, and I did it to be part of the group – ridiculous.

Bed was at ten, lights off at eleven. Everything really was meticulous. And apart from in the therapy itself, you didn't have to think. And you didn't have to do any chores or cook for yourself or anything like that – it was bliss. I just floated off – still off my head, but happy.

I loved some of the characters there and what was meant to be two weeks ended up being four. We had a WhatsApp group going for ages afterwards. Looking back, although I was 'sent to rehab' with the right intentions, it was a difficult one to swallow given me and Adam had struggled more or less by ourselves for years at that point. It wasn't what I needed at the time at all and the idea that you can talk through mental trauma, whilst taking medication that prevents you from feeling anything at all, is absolutely ridiculous.

After rehab, I had to get off all the drugs for good. There's a sentence you don't hear very often.

I am now very health conscious, and this period sparked my interest in alternative healing therapies. I have oxygen therapy, and since the beginning of 2023 I have been privately taking other steps in a bid to resolve my health issues.

Under the guidance of a wonderful Harley Street medical specialist called Dr Khan, I'm receiving a new medical treatment that uses my body's stem cells to combat inflammation in the body and calm down my overactive immune system.

When I arrived at the clinic, I was immediately put at ease by Dr Khan, who has a gentle, kind manner. He told me he listens to patients suffering like me, and said, 'We do want to help people in your position.'

I felt he understood immediately the inflammatory symptoms that have been plaguing me.

After a full consultation and rigorous blood testing, Dr Khan confirmed my symptoms pointed to an autoimmune problem and that whatever was causing it is very similar to Long Covid.

I haven't had Long Covid, but he explained that these sort of autoimmune problems can occur after a virus, and that they can also occur after breast implants, when they're referred to as breast implant syndrome.

He explained gently to me that they can't prove for sure it is caused by breast implants, but that doesn't mean to say they don't believe patients, and they are listening to us.

The symptoms I was experiencing can occur due to any sort of upset in the body, which makes the immune system start attacking your own cells, causing inflammation. Dr Khan explained that inflammation is important to kickstart regeneration and healing, but then it should switch off. If the healing process *doesn't* switch it off, or the inflammation is too aggressive, then it can become chronic and start to cause inflammatory damage to tissues, and you can even develop autoimmunity. In other words, it can turn against your own tissues and your own body, and start creating the sort of problems that I experienced. This is when people start to get respiratory problems; they get neurological problems; they get rheumatoid diseases. All of these are mediated by an immune system raging and going wild in the body.

I started feeling better quite soon after he started injecting the serum and it settled in. And the proof of the pudding is in the eating.

Within a few weeks, I noticed an improvement in my energy levels. For the first time since starting the treatment, I got the tube home rather than a taxi. That evening, I cooked, which I hadn't done in forever. My concentration started to come back, which means I am able to do more. But my health is an ongoing work-in-progress, which I am committed to improving for the sake of myself and our family.

Even my mum says she can't believe the difference in me. It's quite astounding. She noticed that my voice is no longer raspy and croaky, my skin has started to glow again, I have energy and that horrible brain fog has lifted.

It's given me my hope back.

And the beauty of the autologous serum is that it comes from your own body. It's not a drug that you can have reactions to. It won't have side effects because it is derived from your own system. Because it's your own body repairing itself, it's a more natural, safer way to go.

I'm assured the regeneration should carry on for a number of months, so my endpoint is going to be six months to a year down the road. Throughout this period, I'll carry on getting better and Dr Khan will continue to monitor me.

We're all hoping that if what originally caused my condition has gone, and this has been a consequence of breast implants or an infection, then I've now been reset and I should be able to carry on as normal.

I've also been warned that if I was to have implants again, it could trigger the autoimmune problems again, because my body responds in a certain way to breast implants. I would never, no chance.

I really hope that we can get this treatment on to the National Health Service, as it has the potential to save lives. Along with explant surgery.

When I was offered the chance to make a documentary about Breast Implant Illness (BII) for ITV, it felt like a vindication to a degree. Having another medical expert on the subject take me seriously and tell me on record that yes, this was an illness, I wasn't going mad, and what Adam had been saying for years was right, felt very reassuring. Put simply, my implants were poisoning me. Not just me, but it seemed that these types of implants were poisoning countless women who were unwell and being diagnosed with everything except Breast Implant Illness. It's a bit like that awful scene in *The Sixth Sense* where the little girl has to set the camera up to be able to say she's being poisoned without being able to make anybody believe her, while bravely smiling at the outside world and telling them what they want to hear, which is of course that she's feeling much better now. Few doctors wanted to diagnose this as the cause, but I knew there was no longer any doubt what it was and had shed some light on it to other women possibly suffering. I hoped that I might succeed with the planned treatments and fully restore my own health.

My reality prior to that was that I desperately needed ex-plant surgery, these things would have to be removed, and as the date drew closer, I found myself heading off to a place that I would come to call my 'go to'. That place is called Complete Denial. I know I've already mentioned this surgery, but it was such a huge event, that it's important to share my memories of it, no matter how fragmented it may seem.

With the date set and the bags packed, it was almost time to go. Adam was being supportive, and I thought I was ready. We were due to drive to Torquay at 5 a.m. and as the clock ticked past midnight, I knew I wasn't going to go. I didn't want to remain sick. No, of course I wanted to get better, but I was all over the place, jumping from one end of the spectrum to the other. Deep down, I knew the implants had to come out, but I had become so tired and so used to being unwell that I just couldn't face it.

Looking back, I realise how unreasonable it was to expect to Adam to understand. Even the most supportive partner in the world can only take so much of the irrational, illogical behaviour of their other half suddenly appearing to not want to get well – not having the drive for it. How could he get what I was going through when I didn't understand myself? This was as bad as it got between us and, yes, we did separate again for a time, it must've just seemed like I didn't care. In that moment, I decided I wasn't having my implants out, and I wasn't going to explain myself easily, so much so that it might actually have appeared I wanted to keep my breasts the way they were for vanity's sake when that couldn't have been further from the truth.

We separated for a bit again. We didn't see each other properly for a month or so and communicating became very, very difficult. I knew deep down Adam was right and he was justified in what he was doing and saying, but how dare he be a bloke talking about these things as though it wasn't my body about to be cut up. Whereas I know from his point of view, it was just complete frustration that my health was getting worse, and the most important action needed had been kicked into the long grass. The total exhaustion, the instability, all of it was what was making my decisions for me, and it was the start of me feeling like someone else was living my life and I was on the outside looking in.

How I ended up going for the surgery, the surgery itself, and the aftermath are all now somewhat of a blur, but once it was done the first step to getting back to being Healthy Hannah had been taken. What I didn't know was my theoretical mountain really was only a staircase and there was plenty more for me to climb. I was going to have to trek much further and far steeper than I could ever imagine.

After the operation, I felt the clouds gradually beginning to lift, and it felt like I was getting better. Adam and I were in a great place for the first time in a long time so much so that we decided that we would try for another baby. Not long after that, we were pregnant. I was excited and thought we must have turned a big corner. As 2021 became 2022 and the world was starting to talk about the pandemic as some sort of historical event rather than being breaking news, every day we as a family began laying down our plans not knowing what 2022 had in store for us. What the year would bring, we could never have imagined in our worst nightmares.

One night in January, and completely out of the blue, I felt unwell and quickly realised that I was bleeding. It started out as normal bleeding, but after a few hours, it started to get heavier and heavier. Eventually, after bleeding through two bath towels, we had to call the ambulance. I knew that I was having a miscarriage, despite having never had anything like this happen to me before – apart from giving birth, of course. I thought it must be normal, even as I felt myself getting weaker and weaker and noticing Adam getting more and more concerned. He jumped on the phone immediately to the emergency services, desperate for an ambulance and I could hear him almost shouting down the phone as they were telling him that it would take around four hours to get to me.

I could feel myself drifting, hearing his voice in a vacuum

as he tried to tell them that he didn't think I would survive for four hours with the amount of blood that I had lost. I heard him say 'how many pads has she been through?! I didn't know that there was that much blood in the human body,' and it must've been words like that which got them to make me a priority. It was only twenty minutes later the ambulance arrived, and I was on my way to hospital. Around one o'clock in the morning I had an emergency operation to stop the bleeding and the whole traumatic experience melted away briefly as I fell into a long, deep sleep. I didn't know it then, but the miscarriage was the start of me being put firmly back where I started in terms of my poor health.

I was telling myself in the months afterwards that I was OK. Yes, I had a miscarriage. Yes, it had been a shocking experience, but I wasn't going to let it stop me and Adam from planning for another child. Only three months later, with some surprise after the recent trauma, I was confirmed as pregnant again.

We thought that the first miscarriage would be an isolated incident. Then, in August, I had my second miscarriage. While nowhere near as physically traumatic as the first one, in my mind, I couldn't stop thinking that I had lost two children and was struggling to cope physically. I was almost back where I had been at my worst moments of the period leading up to the operation to remove the implants. Surely, I would get past it this time and "get well soon" as the cliche says? Again, we started looking for support and looking for new tools for the kit to cope with what had happened, not once but twice in a matter of months.

In the aftermath of my second miscarriage, I did go looking

for support, for information to help me cope with what had happened to me. In all honesty I couldn't really find anything. As women, we are expected to just get on with it. Miscarriages are seemingly a part of life, they happen every day, and there's a shrug-of-the-shoulders attitude generally from society. The fact is that every experience is different, and my two experiences were at very different ends of the scale. It's a scary moment in life and put in the context of having had – and having again that feeling of it being back – a long-term debilitating illness, I do wonder if digging deeper into personal circumstances might help some women cope and recover more wholly.

Chapter Twelve

Fake News

As a celebrity in the public eye, fake stories in the media are seen as part and parcel of the job.

I am not going to preach on or argue the ethics of that or whether it's right or wrong; it is what it is.

And as they say, it's tomorrow's chip paper.

But when stories that are blatantly untrue cause hurt to other people going about their lives and minding their own business then I take umbrage, and I want to use this chapter to correct some half-truths and smears.

At the start of 2023 I was astonished to open a well-known paper and see that they'd run a false headline calling me homeless. The person who wrote that story has written other fabricated half-baked tales about me in the past that I've let go of as it's a waste of energy trying to fight them.

This time I couldn't. Some months before the story was published, a woman had come to work for me, not as a PA but an office/home assistant of sorts. She would declutter things and she'd help me in the house with organisation, documents and other menial tasks I'd been putting off doing.

Things started to get a little strange. She told me she was bringing a planner out onto the market, and she knew how much I loved them. This was true – I'm not anymore, but for a time I became a bit obsessed with planners. So I was enthusiastic, and I said, in another life I might have brought one out myself.

Shortly after that, she came to me with the offer of collaborating in her business. I politely said I was honoured to be asked, and thought it was a nice gesture. I said it sounded very interesting, and that I was excited to read it.

I didn't say no straight away – but I didn't say yes either. I just said I'd look it over. And then she forwarded me a contract that didn't have the greatest terms. I kindly explained that it wasn't right for me at that time – I said no, in a nice way.

She reacted calmly, which was a relief; you never know how people will handle rejection. But that wasn't the last we heard of her.

Her and Adam also had a fractured relationship, which didn't help things. She started to do the opposite of what we asked her to do and, over time, it felt like she was slowly but surely turning our home into her house.

Then in the winter of 2022, not long after she had stopped working for me, I got a call from my agent.

'Hi, Hannah, this is odd. I've had a call from the *Sun* saying someone had sold them a story about you being homeless and they're giving you a chance to comment. I've told them it's totally false and to desist printing.'

My reaction was one of bewilderment. It was rubbish, and I had no idea where it came from.

Over the next two weeks my agent took more of these calls, threatening to run this made-up story every Saturday unless we gave them a sit-down interview, and each time we'd tell them *no, piss off, we don't give a shit*, and they wouldn't run it.

Late in December, my agent got a call saying somebody had contacted the paper with photos of us.

Someone had sneakily taken pictures of us moving house and our stuff in the street, then sold them to the *Sun* as evidence that we were homeless down-and-outs, living on the streets.

They continued to threaten to publish the story without any comment from me, despite us sending a legal letter saying we had Land Registry documents proving that we were homeowners, and that the story was categorically not true. It did nothing to get them to see sense and drop this non-story.

They persisted, even offering to make it positive if I co-operated and gave them an interview, telling us that they'd make it about our other business ventures and not mention homelessness.

Eventually we caved in, as at least this way we could correct their premise – and we still hoped that they'd drop it when I explained that it was not true.

We explained the truth of the situation, that we were between homes and were carrying out renovation work on our family property. In the meantime, because of the dust and mess, we were staying in a temporary house and going back and forth to work on our own house in Middlesex, which WE OWN.

The landlord of our house we were living in was a nice guy and he had a bit of an emergency and needed to sell his house; we didn't want to stand in his way, so we went to dog-sit at a friend's house while he was away. When he came back from holiday, we moved back into our newly renovated house.

So we spent a night going through their proposed story, saying, 'Do not put that in. Do not put that in. It's not true.' And what was their headline? 'S Club Hannah Homeless', with the tag line 'people think we're millionaires but we have nowhere to live . . . ' That was categorically not true, and they knew it.

I didn't see the story until the day after they put it online, and Adam had kept it from being on the front page from me for 3 or 4 days so that I was able to have a good night's sleep.

He knew I would explode – and he was right – so he tried to protect me until I got the first call and by that time I'd got into a place where I could laugh about it.

The reporter in question had sat there, looked me dead in the eye and told me to my face that there would be no mention of homelessness – just as the paper had said on the phone.

We left and everything was lovely. But he knew all along what he was going to do, because they just wanted to use the picture they'd bought, so it appeared more real.

They wrote that we were living in an office – but that was just our café premises, where we'd put all the children's play stuff; we would go there in the day as the builders worked. I haven't spoken open out our café much, but it's an important place for us.

We also had a couple of camp beds in there so they could nap, and we'd stored a few of our possessions there to protect them from the dust at home. Our place was just so dusty and dirty with the renovation project, anything left there might have been ruined. It was so dusty that just dragging a piece of furniture across the floor would make it filthy. The café was just up the road from where we were doing the work, so it made sense to keep some of our best furniture there.

I wanted to sue, but we agreed that we'd had enough stress for one year already.

I also want to address the part of the article that said our landlord gave us two days' notice. Our landlord, Lester, was so lovely, and I can't let that go because it made him look to be the bad guy when he had done nothing wrong but be the perfect gentleman. He even trimmed our bloody trees for us! They didn't name him, but it's still wrong that they can still get away with that, and it's infuriating that people still read tabloids and believe them.

When the story was published, friends and family were calling asking why we hadn't told them we were struggling.

That article was an insult to people who are really homeless and having to live on the streets because there's no help or resources available and usually through no fault of their own.

It made it look like I was laughing at them, and bragging about my own situation being intolerable when it was categorically false. It felt like the height of hypocrisy – I am a long way from being homeless, and it's a serious problem in the UK today.

Chapter Thirteen

Family Ties

I was living in St Margaret's in south-west London, having come out of my relationship with Andrew about three months previously.

A friend recommended a personal trainer who was brilliant at helping with flexibility and writing nutritional plans as I wanted to improve my flexibility for yoga and weighted exercises were making me feel stiff.

She gave me Adam's number and he said he would be happy to give a complimentary assessment.

I drove over to his gym in Marylebone in the pouring rain but couldn't find it. I called him to say I wasn't sure if I was at the right place, and if he could he pop out to find me, as it was off the main road.

At that point he came out of the gym and started walking towards my car, fifty metres away, and I jumped out and started walking towards him. It was lashing down but I barely noticed.

I don't know what it was, but I will always remember that; it was just such a lovely moment. Even though I turned up soaked, I saw this kind man trying to help out, searching for me in the rain.

I wasn't looking for or expecting anything from it, but we were completely drawn to each other from the first meeting, and both just living in the moment.

I found him devastatingly attractive at first sight, but then there were other things I liked too. It was almost like a closeness; it was more than just wanting to get to know him. I would never have spent that many hours with somebody in a gym if I didn't fancy them.

We had so much in common. He was three months out of a long relationship, as I was, which we spoke about a lot. We both loved looking after our health and working out, and it was just a very healthy start. We were both five months teetotal, so it was just a really, really pure time.

Sometimes you meet someone in a bar and it's all a bit chaotic; this was the opposite of that. It was peaceful and calm and it took my breath away a bit because I was like, maybe this is how life could be; maybe this is what we could have.

It was quite breathtaking in that sense – we were able to be totally ourselves with each other with no artifice. And he embodied traits that I've never experienced before in anybody that I'd been with – no disrespect to any of my previous partners – he just had qualities that were good for me, and gave me a sense of balance. He made me feel like I was home and safe.

Obviously we trained and then we trained again and then we trained again, and our sessions turned from what should have been one hour to sometimes five. Now we weren't always exercising in that time; if we'd worked out for five hours a session I'd have been a walking stick insect, so we'd sit down with our healthy supplements and talk.

The gym was open twenty-four hours a day, so I could drop in whenever, and our first kiss was in the gym car park at 3 a.m.

After that there was no overthinking or questioning myself if it was the right thing to do – I just knew with complete certainty he felt exactly the same way about me as I did about him.

From then on we were smitten and joined at the hip, and I knew he was the future father of my children.

I've already discussed our break-up, but after all the drama of the implants, when we got back together in 2017 we went on a very long holiday to Costa Rica and just did lots of healthy stuff.

In 2018 I decided to do a charity boxing match to see what I was capable of. This was my opportunity to find out how well I was doing and to push myself. But during the training I started feeling very emotional, crying and just acting out of character. Three days after the fight, I found out I was pregnant with our eldest daughter Taya, which would explain a lot.

Adam had moved to St Margaret's by this point, and his then thirteen-year-old daughter Leah had come to live with us. Navigating the role of step-mother has been hard at times but richly rewarding. There was a time Leah and I struggled to get on, which tied in with my illness and surgery. Leah knew we wanted a family, but I can only imagine how hard it was, being a daddy's girl – and his only girl, all her life – to have to share him with me. And all while navigating and getting to grips with being a teenager and raging hormones.

It's a joy to witness the beautiful, special bond she has with her father. Watching them together, and how Adam parents and cares for her, was a huge factor in my falling in love with him. She is his world and always will be.

I just wish I could have been a better step-mother from the outset. Having a bit more experience I know what I would've done differently. Because you learn as you go. I think the problem was that I started to retreat within myself because I feared saying the wrong thing and upsetting her. And she didn't understand why I wasn't communicating with her better – from her perspective it must have felt like I didn't want her there. The headspace I started occupying became extremely unhealthy for me, and probably for her too. It just wasn't working.

Everyone's position was extremely different during that time. Adam was caught in the middle. My body was changing, and I was getting upset about things that probably wouldn't have bothered me before. The atmosphere in the house completely changed with Leah being there and it was a tough time. Pregnancies are difficult anyway, and I didn't know how to handle it and/or how to control my emotions.

I wasn't flying off the handle, but I'd go quiet a lot over silly stuff. Shortly after giving birth to Taya, I moved out for a bit and got a flat on my own; I just desperately needed some time apart, and with all the tension that had built up between us in the house, I thought we could all benefit from a break.

By going away, I could come back to myself and not be troubled by unnecessary overthinking. The house wasn't big enough for everybody, especially with a baby. I had to give myself space to reset.

There's always stuff to learn, and that there are always parts of yourself that've never grown up. And that was what happened when Leah came into my life. I had not dealt with some of my own childhood traumas, and it triggered me.

I'm going to refer again here to those formative years I missed out on that I suspect hindered my development and life experience. My very insular existence of being around just the same six people for five odd years, plus an entourage and fame at a young age.

I would say that I probably didn't have the confidence to step into that role of a stepmother without having been a mother first and struggled with the concept. I guess it's a form of Imposter Syndrome and knowing what I know now, I should've just embraced it and given my best instead of overthinking it, after all, what else can you do anyway? If I didn't have the emotional tools to navigate the situation, how on earth could I expect Leah to?

I'm not saying being criticised all the time is healthy, but learning to cope with a degree of criticism is useful. I do think things come into your life that may well be extremely hard to go through emotionally, and when I was pregnant and living with Adam and Leah, maybe I didn't have the emotional tools to deal with it.

And I've found that I've learned to enjoy the simple things again with my kids. Happiness is the journey and not a destination, 'n' all that.

Knowing what I know now, I could have handled things so much better with Leah. But we're still here and we're now very close; she is my daughter now, afterall.

*

Leah writes:

Hannah and I say we're quite similar in many ways and we shared some interests, so we've bonded over that.

As I've been raised by Hannah and my dad for several years now, I've grown up to share a lot of their traits, especially in terms of my nutrition. I'm also very organised, just like Hannah. I'd say my humour is quite close to Hannah's too.

It hasn't been hard having a famous step-mother because when I first met her I was so young, around nine and I didn't actually know anything about the band at all.

I knew the song 'Reach', but besides that, I didn't really know anything.

So when my dad told me how they got together, and that he was training her, I was so intrigued that he might be dating a celebrity that I started looking up her songs and trying to learn them.

And then I started telling my friends, who thought it was quite cool. There was only one situation that I struggled with, which was when someone told my teacher, who started singing S Club songs to me in front of the class. That was the lowest point, and I was so embarrassed I wanted the ground to swallow me up.

The teachers play Hannah's music on the school bus to Taya, which is cute, but when you're a bit older, hearing your teacher do that makes you cringe.

I was really looking forward to the tour and watching Hannah. My boyfriend and I had bought tickets for it, as I'd gone to the reunion tour in 2012 and that was a really good night.

I don't really see any of the friends that I had from the time when I found out about Dad dating Hannah, and the friends that I have now aren't interested. It's only been a hazard once when I was bunking off school and got papped – the teachers had thought I was at home ill.

It's great living with Hannah now because I go to her for advice on nearly everything – from boys to health and work. Now that I have a boyfriend, there's not really a need to talk about boys to her anymore, but I know if there is a problem I can go to either her or my dad. My dad's pretty chill with those sorts of conversations. But I just speak to them both and they pretty much know the ins and outs of my life.

When I had some private family issues going on, I did speak to Hannah a lot about it because she can relate on some sort of level. I think she'd witnessed a lot of what I struggled with when I was younger so she knew what I was going through.

I had grown up with a stepdad, so I'd already had that experience of second parenting. Sometimes I guess I felt lonely in that I don't have a brother or sister that I could fully relate to because my first sibling was born when I was four and a half; I'm now one of five, but there's still that big age gap between me and all of the others. So when I had difficulties with any of my four parents, there wasn't a sibling to talk to.

If I was to have kids, I would plan to stay with the person that I have them with, but that's quite common now, to be honest.

My mum got pregnant at twenty, so my parents were really young and I believe that played a large part as to why it didn't work out for them. Either way, I think having me, helped them both mature and grow up, in turn realising what they both wanted, which was to separate. It did and sometimes still does have a big impact on me, but in the best way, because I wouldn't be who I am without my story; it shapes who you are.

And I think there are lot of situations I could easily deal with now because of my experiences. Now that I'm older and an adult, I try and deal with stuff more on my own, but I also feel like if I wanted to talk to Hannah about anything, I would a hundred per cent feel like I could.

Hannah is really cool with her tattoos, and she says I am allowed one, so I think I might have one of Lola, my little Chihuahua.

I was quite young when Hannah was not well – it was the beginning of my relationship with her. I didn't know she'd had breast implants. And I actually remember seeing her in a bra. I said to Dad, 'Oh my God, her boobs are amazing.'

It must have been hard for Hannah when I first came to live with them, because she didn't know me that well. To be comfortable, to be that vulnerable in front of a young girl would be tough – I'd find it difficult, anyway.

And so there were points where my dad would be upstairs with Hannah and then I would just kind of wait for him to come down the stairs. This was hard for me, because I didn't really know what was going on. I was only eleven and I wanted to help but would be told I couldn't go near her because she was so ill with this mystery illness.

And when my dad kind of became her carer, things became even more difficult. This was the person that he was in love with, and he was trying so hard just to keep her standing up and functioning. I think it definitely took a toll on him as well, which I struggled with a lot as my dad is like my world.

So, it was hard to see both Hannah and my dad going downhill. I mean, as a man, there's only so much my dad will let on to in terms of emotion. But he was clearly having a challenging time.

When Hannah moved out with my baby sister there were quite a few negative things that happened between my dad and Hannah in terms of them not being together. Naturally, I put my dad first, and I'd try and look at it from his perspective and be there for him, but it was awful to see him upset.

Once she had the breast implants removed, I couldn't wait for her to be better so we could be a family again and do fun things like we had used to.

There was a period of adjusting as Hannah was in her thirties and she was almost like an elderly person, struggling to live.

I mean, it's impossible to comprehend that from a young age. I guess I just blocked out the situation for self-preservation. Of course, it was hard for everyone involved. But it was so moving to see both my dad and Hannah being interviewed on *This Morning* about what had happened with her health.

I was backstage and I was very happy and excited about it, watching my dad be able to talk about the situation as well as Hannah because he went through it as well. My dad plays a huge part in her story, it was just nice to see him be able to have at least that moment of recognition, because he did everything for Hannah to keep her going.

I didn't get to grow up seeing my mum and dad together and therefore never got to really have that love story to look up to.

So to see my dad put his life on standstill to care so much for someone was lovely, and showed to everyone how he felt about Hannah.

As a result there are a lot of things in my own relationship now that either I'll tolerate or not, and I've learned that from seeing their relationship. I know that love is a wonderful thing and now I'm getting to experience that love with my boyfriend.

Chapter Fourteen

Crossroads

E very mum knows a mum with a horror birth story. I had all these ideas for a natural birth with my firstborn, but such things rarely go to plan.

My contractions started at the house. Everything was kind of lovely to start with. Music was on, I got in the bath, and was very comfortable. But when I got out of the bath, the contractions shot to a whole other level of pain, and had to go to the hospital.

The cab journey was just hell. I've never experienced pain like it. By the time I got to the hospital, they knew I was coming in as I had been screaming outside.

It was so painful. I was just like a crazed animal – it's indescribable, and I was bussed through a shocked reception room of horrified people and through to the birthing suite.

I wouldn't recommend epidurals as my back hasn't been right ever since, but the pain was so unbelievable I begged them for one.

I began pushing as instructed, but she got stuck halfway and then, all of a sudden, about ten people came rushing into the room. I remember watching a lady crouch down between my legs, brandishing a mightily sharp pair of large scissors, and before I could even ask her what the hell she was intending to do with those, blood was spurting everywhere.

The most frightening thing was that she did it so quickly. It wasn't like she knelt down and looked at it closely, taking her time. She just bent down, snipped it and carried on, almost in a single motion.

I don't blame you if you're crossing your legs and wincing as you read this. I still do, and I was the one who had the procedure!

I lost a lot of blood.

And then they pulled Taya out with forceps. At first she sported a temporary conehead as she had been squashed by the forceps. The poor little girl had this massive misshapen long head, which thankfully changed shortly after – although we do have the pictures!

My second birth was far less dramatic. I had a lovely pregnancy. I just felt very fit throughout pregnancy from working out an hour a day. I also had minimal morning sickness with Tora. After what happened with Taya they recommended a C-section.

We really would love another baby but sadly, since Tora, I've had two miscarriages as I said, so it's been pretty full on. But we're not going to let the miscarriages put us off.

I lost them both at the same point, which was eleven and a half weeks. It was not only very traumatic and emotionally draining, but also physically traumatic. The second one was life-threatening, and I find it hard to talk about it. And so to go through a third miscarriage back-to-back would not be fun.

I know you can't approach life like that, but at the same

time I didn't want to go straight into it again. I am sure we will get there again soon, or at least try. In an ideal world I would like to have a little bit more of a break if I am still lucky enough to be able to conceive again.

As for marriage, whilst I do embrace the traditional roles, I've never been too bothered about being able to say, 'I'm officially married', in the conventional sense. I think we'll get each other rings soon, because we are already married in our hearts. I never imagined it as a child, but when we end up living in an exotic place, which we will actually make happen relatively soon, then I can see us getting married, or having some sort of ceremony, on a beach. But it will be low-key, small and probably just us, some family and close friends. Unless Hello! magazine wants to buy the rights – joke! Barefoot, on a beach, casual dress, in the sun with the kids. Job done. Me becoming the little wifey, 'her indoors' – that always makes me laugh, saying it out loud. Yeah, why not!

My life has changed so much in the last few years. I'm now a busy mum of two with a possible future third child on the way, and my career as an actress has taken a back seat.

COVID-19 hit during that time of change for me, which was obviously strange for everybody. In lockdown, I began studying holistic health and now I plan to work as a holistic healer with my own centre and health café called Earth & Fire. I first got the idea in 2017 when Adam and I were in Costa Rica; we went to a café called Cafe Mono Congo every morning for coffees and juices. I became engrossed with making tinctures and different sorts of foods, and studying and cooking the stuff that has always excited me – fermented foods, sauerkraut, kimchi, healing broths and all that sort of stuff.

So Covid was quite a good time for me in terms of learning. I always feel more alive when eating and cooking healthily, and I'm sure many people feel the same.

In my past career I never really had time to go into those other areas that were of interest to me. And I think during the lockdowns, the things that really mattered to me did come to the forefront a lot more.

I felt a strong sort of need to be my own doctor as much as I could to prevent myself from getting ill or anything happening because of my journey and the health issues I've had, and I want to pass that knowledge on. The Academy of Healing Nutrition is where I did my course, and I can highly recommend it. Thank you again!

We have been working hard to make the café come to life. We were set to open last year, but things have taken a lot longer than we had anticipated. This year has been hugely stressful and all-encompassing, and to that end I am questioning whether this the right place for us to live. Both Adam and I have coincidentally lived, strangely enough, in Barcelona, at the same time in the late 90s early 00s.

We haven't decided whether we are going to open a café now in the end, the last twelve months have taken their toll and running a very hands-on business may not be the best thing for my health right now.

If you asked me to google a picture of myself, the results would churn out somebody who could be homeless, who could be famous, who could be ill, or grieving, or could be all sorts of things, I wouldn't have been surprised by any of those results. That is who I really have been over the last three years, apart from the homeless bit, of course . . .

I have been very, very unwell. Now that I have been able to write this down. I know that I still have a determination and an inner voice that ensures that I will always face every day to feel as well as I can, no matter what, for the children, for Adam, and for me.

I have made huge strides this year in returning to optimal health and fitness using some of the most cutting-edge treatments from some wonderful people. I want to completely eradicate the isolated days of fatigue and I really feel that this has allowed me to believe that I'm getting through it and making that happen. The light at the end of the tunnel is glowing brightly right now.

As winter arrived, Adam and I house sat for a friend of ours in Virginia Water. This wasn't going to be a normal house sit as it were, the house in question is enormous with countless rooms, huge gardens and on the face of it a fun and exciting place to be with our two girls. Little did we know what an absolute nightmare this was going to turn into. It was the 22nd of December 2022, mere days before Christmas.

That was when we found out that the former employee of ours was peddling a story about us, somehow, being homeless. This was false, as well as most of what she was telling this one journalist in particular. I would need an entire book to cover what I think of certain members of the media . . . I have a huge amount of respect for so many people who work in the media, whether that's a newspaper, on TV, online or whatever. The majority have integrity and want to write about interesting people with interesting lives and interesting stories.

Unfortunately, a small percentage of those people don't

care whether what they write is true or not so long as they get the headline. Surely today, it's been proven repeatedly that telling lies in print is not acceptable. Does it take the downfall of another newspaper for them to realize that what they write has consequences? In our case, because of a malicious allegation out of revenge, coupled with a newspaper being prepared to print some of those allegations, we found ourselves on the radar of social services, an absolutely ridiculous situation to be in, totally unjustified. And as you will read, it became the backbone of yet another crisis, not just for me this time, but directly for Adam and the children as well.

So back to the house, we were all having fun together in one of the rooms when Felan, Hannah's manager, called us. He told us about someone trying to sell a homeless story on us, and of course that completely destroyed the mood. We were discussing who it could be, and I was pretty distraught at this point. Anyway, Tora ran out of the kitchen and into the living room whilst we followed on with drinks, when we heard her crying. I ran through to the living room whilst Adam finished filling up the Berkey water filter. The scene that I came upon in the living room will stay with me forever. Tora was standing on the couch, her right eyelid horrifically lacerated and probably the worst facial injury I've ever seen. I carried her through to the kitchen and started to go into shock whilst Adam phoned an ambulance, trying to stay calm but visibly shaken. He changed her and mopped up all the blood so she wouldn't see it and it cause her to start panicking. Only one of us could accompany her in the ambulance, so I stayed with Taya and waited for my friend to come around in the car so we could follow them to the hospital.

It seemed like an eternity before we got to the hospital because they went to an initial hospital A&E and then were transferred on to a hospital with a specialist eye unit, and Adam told us that there was a specialist surgeon, a lovely Greek lady, who would do the surgery and that she was not going to be able to do it till the following day because she required an exploratory surgery to examine the damage and ensure the eyeball was 'still intact'. That statement still reminds me of how worried sick we were back then. We were told she was the best and the only person who could do the surgery in the south east at the time, such was the intricacy of that particular procedure. So we settled in to comfort Tora as best we could with what we thought were supportive members of the nursing staff and doctors whilst we awaited the first surgery. About fifteen minutes before Tora was to go in to review the condition of the eye, one of the nurses came in, and asked Adam if she could have a word with him outside. I thought nothing of it as he left. What I didn't know was that as soon as he left the room, the police were waiting for him and arrested him. Tora needed emergency plastic surgery to piece her eyelid back together and in equal measure she needed her father at her side. What was already a terrible situation had ramped up to something unbelievable.

I found out that Adam was no longer in the hospital – I was told five minutes later by a nurse. Unbelievably, he was in the police station because the police and some of the hospital staff felt that it was more likely that he was responsible for the injury. What we later found out was that they suspected both of us and took the decision to leave one of us with our daughter. While our little girl was lying in a hospital bed, we were waiting for the potentially life-changing news of whether she'd lost sight in one eye.

We had to attend a Zoom call alongside people from the police, social services and the hospital. The nurse who attended when we arrived at the hospital, to our great relief, immediately stated that in her opinion, based on her many years of experience, there was simply no way that we could have been responsible for what happened and, while at the time it was something that should have been rightly considered, it was very clear that it couldn't possibly be the cause. What we were essentially being accused of was near on impossible and, while there was no evidence to pinpoint exactly what had actually happened, our belief – stated over and over again at every stage – was that one of the dogs we were looking after had jumped up on Tora in excitement as they ran between the rooms and had accidentally swept his foot across her face, with one of his claws causing the injury. It really would not have taken much work at all on the part of the social services people to reach the same conclusion.

It's truly frightening to think that someone with absolutely zero evidence can paint a picture like that which influences someone being arrested and locked up while their daughter lies in a hospital bed, waiting for major surgery. It felt like persecution, like one of those police states that people talk about. When they finally let Adam out on bail, they would not give him back his phone, and throughout the entire twelve hours did not give him any updates on how Tora was doing. Now, eight months later, as of writing this, they still have not returned his phone. Our complaints with all the services are ongoing at this time.

We are eternally grateful to the surgeon for the work she did on Tora's eye. It was a success, and she made a full recovery, at least physically. It's hard to know the full impact, given the way we were treated as a couple and as parents may or may not have had on her subliminally. We all know that children pick up on their parents' emotions – a daughter knows her mother probably better than most other people, so she must have been lying there, dealing with her injury, missing her dad and quite frightened. Honestly. I don't think I can ever forgive the people responsible, although we've made every effort to forget about it and them as quickly as possible. Being able to do that, it transpired, was not going to be very easy. Despite the testimony of the nurse, social services were more inclined to believe that there was no smoke without fire. We were told that, incredibly, we would have to live in accommodation where two other responsible adults were present 100% of the time while they continued their investigation. This was adding insult to serious injury and bearing in mind my gradual decline in health generally, I was really beginning to despair.

Writing this down is the first time I've revisited it, and it becomes even more shocking the more I write. Almost immediately, we began demanding answers from the authorities and all these months later we still have none really. I'm sure in the fullness of time we will get some sort of justice, and if anything, it might go towards stopping this type of thing happening again or to other families. And even when the newspapers were running so many stories, it did not leak out. I don't know if they were simply embarrassed, realising they had made a serious mistake, but I think they should have been.

Ultimately, the only thing that really mattered was Tora's eyesight.

As we moved into January 2023 my health was seriously deteriorating. The idea of the band reforming looked like it might be on the cards, but the homeless story had made the front page of the newspaper and the shock of what happened to Tora was only just beginning to sink in. All the nonsense with the police and social services was also in the background. Meanwhile, our plans for growing our business, developing the premises and all that went with that were underway. I wanted to contribute and help Adam and I really didn't want him to think that I was on the path back to being seriously ill. It's likely that because I wanted to present that it was having the opposite effect.

I was just desperate to get back to being the Hannah that I was before any of this ever happened. I wanted to be ready to take the world on again in 2023, and as the conversations were taking place about an S Club 7 reunion, they were paling into insignificance by comparison with the thought, *hey, are you ever going to be 100% well again?* Every time I actually managed to get out of the house, feeling like I could do something, I would be home with a cold or something and be weighed down by everything going on in almost no time. So even while things were happening all around me, planning for the tour, deep down, I wasn't even sure if I would survive to get to the first show. The stress was getting to me.

I had suffered a major illness, on top of which I had two births, the two miscarriages with no aftercare, so even though I was following a regime of health and fitness and eating well, wanting to get back on stage and taking the world on seemed a bit of a mountain to climb. The Hannah I really longed to be would have to wait until I felt somewhat better.

Meanwhile, Adam was dealing with the real me, the not-so-well-all-the-time me, while he was working and looking after the kids. And that brings us full circle on the timeline to the beginning of this book!

Now we are at a crossroads – we have one eye on Costa Rica, our promised land, I suspect . . .

One thing I can say for certain is that I won't be screaming out for more on the S Club tour!

And now I am sad to say that the time has come to say so long and farewell to you, dear reader. I hope you enjoyed my little story of life, and thank YOU for reading this.

And if you've struggled with any of the issues raised in this book, please turn to the recommended guidance numbers listed in the Resources section.

Love always,
Hannah x

Afterword

I f I may, I'd like to end on a positive note and share a little insight into the latest project we've been working on. Because despite what has happened in the past and recently, I am excited and energised for the next phase of my life.

In 2017, we went travelling to Costa Rica and encountered not only the most beautiful country but the most amazingly friendly people. We just knew we had to return some day, and perhaps, on a more permanent basis. We have spent a long time looking, researching and learning about the process from people with experience in this field, and we've found a large parcel of land. We are planning to set up a community living space there, a farm, as well as yoga and wellness retreats and eventually a fully functioning resort and eco town.

The plan is to be as alternative as possible, and mindful and respectful of the planet, wildlife and others with every aspect of its day-to-day existence.

We want art studio tree houses to run courses, rooftop yoga under the stars, outdoor hot tubs and spas. There are twenty waterfalls on site with their own natural plunge pools to swim in and it is bordered by the rainforest on one side and the Pacific Ocean the other. Paradise.

I think that amongst other lessons over the last few years, I've learnt that life can be tragically short, possessions are overrated, as well as happiness not being a tangible commodity. My health permitting, we're going to make our dreams become a reality. I hasten to add that we will be looking for people to join our community and enrich it, as well as people to come and help in a host of different aspects, and welcome all like-minded people to come and check it out. So if you think it sounds like something you'd be interested in, check back soon and we'll have more information available!

For the first time in a long time, my heart is full of hope for the future – whatever it may hold.

Pura vida.

Acknowledgements

With the risk of this sounding like an acceptance speech, there are many people I'd like to express my gratitude to.

The past year has been exceptionally tough, coming after what I felt had been a tough three or four years prior, what with lockdowns and two tiny children, but these tough times are the only circumstances that show you who's in your corner.

As tough as it's been recently, those tiny two, Taya and Tora have managed to make us smile no matter what. They are unbelievably strong characters (and naughty) and I wouldn't want them any other way!

I'd like to start by thanking all the S Club fans. Without your following and continued support, there would be no one to read this in the first place.

All of you who turned out to see me at the comic cons repeatedly, and who I've shared many laughs with, a big thank you to all of you.

My management team, Martin and Felan at Bold, have probably been that fragile thread between navigating extended periods of stress and just having a complete nervous breakdown.

To Joelle, Christina, Sharmaine, Millie, Emily and all the

team at Dialogue for making this happen and accommodating my faltering at times, due to health issues and other unforeseen obstacles.

To Jaine, my book agent, my Little Miss Fix It, who went the extra mile to help me get my health back on track when life came and knocked me for six.

My mum, for all that she's done and for her hours of trawling through all our old family photos for a suitable selection to bring this book to life. Thanks, Mum!

To my dad, taking this walk down memory lane has been a reminder of all that you've done for me and the sound advice you've given me over the years.

My brother Stuart, his wife, Jenna and my sister Tanya and her husband Arber, we managed to fit a holiday in over the summer together and it was lovely to see you all. I will endeavour not to let the literal distances between us allow it to be so long before the next adventure!

Adam's sister, Kate, her partner (other)Adam, who also helped us considerably with our Twickenham project and my Adam's mum "Grandma Suze".

Adams sister Sam and Father Paul. Thank you for all your help and support getting through Tora's accident earlier this year.

My childhood BFFs, Jude and Anneliese. The continued periods of stress over the last few years, and us being a fair distance apart have come between us spending more time together and we need to put that right as soon as humanly possible. Love you two!

Gene, Tracy, Olivia, Billy, Beau, Katie, Riess and Val for

their newfound friendship, help and support over the last few years. Words cannot express how thankful we are as a family.

Our good friends and another important part of our work in Twickenham, Steve "Pablo" Reddings, his partner, Kel and his right-hand man, Brian.

Geoff and Heidi, Geoff very kindly helped us out last Christmas by letting us use his office space . . . and then got dragged into the unfounded homeless story which we unreservedly apologise for, and the additional stress it caused him.

A shout out to our new neighbours who have made us feel so welcome, Barry, Tracy & Emily, Diane & Bob, Jeremy and John.

Thank you to our friend Pete, always there when the smoke clears, in more ways than one.

Thanks to Sheridan for all the memories, I still look back on them fondly.

Thank you NYMT for shaping my direction and the opportunities I was afforded.

Last but not least, my partner in life, Adam. Your perseverance, patience, holding the fort and keeping me on track when things got tough, you kept me going. You and I both know this book wouldn't have happened without you.

And finally, again, the biggest thank you to all of you in the different ways you've all been integral parts of our lives because the people mentioned above, are the ones who got us through the stories in this book in one piece. Onwards and upwards, looking forward to our next chapter!

Hannah xx

Resources
When You Need a Little
Extra Help

Nobody is infallible from the knocks and scrapes of life. We all go through things and sometimes you may need a little extra help outside of friends and family.

During this book I've opened up to you about the devastating events that have happened to me in my life.

If you are going through, or have gone through, loss, miscarriage, breast implant illness, relationship breakdowns, or other trauma, this page gives a list of recommendations that can offer that support.

Never be afraid to ask for help. Take care of yourself.

All numbers and information below is accurate at time of writing this book, but feel free to check online, as information may have changed.

Samaritans – a UK-founded international charity providing support for those in emotional distress or at risk of suicide.

They are available any time, day or night and you can call then any time, from any phone for FREE on 116 123.

Help with grief

Cruse Bereavement Support
This service helps those going through one of the most painful times in life – bereavement.

Their team of trained volunteers can support you in all aspects of grief to make sense of how you're feeling right now – 0808 808 1677

Sudden Bereavement Helpline – 0800 2600 400
10am to 4pm, Monday to Friday – immediate support

Child Bereavement UK – 0800 02 88840 Helpline is open 9–5pm

Grief Talk – 0808 802 0111 for free support Monday to Friday 9am–5pm
For more help and advice visit the www.thegoodgrief trust.org/

Bereavement Advice Centre offers practical advice (9am–5pm) – 0800 634 9494

Or the **Bereavement Trust** offers up emotional and practical advice from (6pm–10pm) – 0800 435 455

Miscarriage and loss of a baby

The charity Tommy's have midwives, who are trained in bereavement support, on their dedicated pregnancy line on 0800 014 7800 (Monday to Friday, 9am to 5pm), or email them at midwife@tommys.org.

Sands also offer a free confidential helpline for anyone affected by pregnancy loss or the death of a baby – 0808 164 3332 10am–3pm Monday to Friday daytimes and 6pm–9pm Tuesday to Thursday evenings.

The Miscarriage Association offers support and information to anyone affected by miscarriage, ectopic or molar pregnancy.
Helpline: 01924 200799
Staffed Monday to Friday 9am–4pm
Email: info@miscarriageassociation.org.uk
Website: miscarriageassociation.org.uk

Struggling with drug or alcohol addiction

DrugFam gives Drug and Alcohol addiction advice. Call 0300 888 3853

The helpline line is available between 9am and 9pm seven days a week.

For painkiller addiction contact PAIN – The Painkiller Addiction Information Network. Visit:
www.painkillerfree.co.uk/contact-us/Painkiller

Relationships

For help with the breakdown of a relationship and other advice visit www.relate.org.uk/get-help

Breast Implant Illness

If you have breast implant(s) and notice any lumps, swellings or distortions in breasts, neck or armpits you should see your GP or implant surgeon in the first instance.

An information pack for patients to learn more about Breast Implant Illness can be found at www.baaps.org.uk/_userfiles/pages/files/bii_information.pdf

BAPRAS offers up advice on possible complications from breast augmentation. Visit www.bapras.org.uk/public/patient-information/surgery-guides/breast-augmentation/what-complications-can-occur

About the author

Hannah Spearritt is an actor and singer. She shot into stardom aged 17 when she joined pop group S Club 7.

During a five-year reign, the group had four UK number one singles and a UK number one album. Famed for their strong late-1990s pop sound, they recorded four studio albums, released eleven singles and went on to sell over fourteen million albums worldwide.

During the course of her time with the band, S Club 7 won two BRIT Awards – in 2000 for British breakthrough act and in 2002, for Best British Single. In 2001, the group earned the Record of the Year award.

After disbanding in 2003, Hannah moved into acting, spending time in Hollywood and starring on TV dramas – *Primeval*, where she portrayed the role of Abby Maitland, *EastEnders* and *Casualty*.

Bringing a book from manuscript to what you are reading is a team effort.

Renegade Books would like to thank everyone who helped to publish *Facing the Music* in the UK.

Editorial
Joelle Owusu-Sekyere

Contracts
Megan Phillips
Amy Patrick
Anne Goddard
Bryony Hall

Design
Bekki Guyatt
Linda Silverman

Audio
Ellie Wheeldon

Sales
Caitriona Row
Dominic Smith

Frances Doyle
Hannah Methuen
Lucy Hine
Toluwalope Ayo-Ajala

Production
Narges Nojoumi

Publicity
Millie Seaward

Marketing
Emily Moran

Operations
Kellie Barnfield
Millie Gibson
Sameera Patel
Sanjeev Braich